The SALMON
Cookbook

The SALMON *Cookbook*

TERESA KAYE

a Salamander book

Published by Salamander Books Limited
LONDON

A SALAMANDER BOOK

© Salamander Books Ltd, 1994

Distributed in Canada by Cavendish Books Inc.,
Unit 5, 801 West 1st Street,
North Vancouver, B.C. V7P 1A4.
Phone (604) 985-2969.

ISBN 0 86101 774 9

CREDITS

COMMISSIONING EDITOR: *Will Steeds*
EDITOR: *Miranda Spicer*
DESIGN: *The Design Revolution, Brighton*
PHOTOGRAPHER: *Simon Butcher*
HOME ECONOMIST: *Wendy Dines*
STYLIST: *Hilary Guy*
COLOR SEPARATION: *P & W Graphics Pte Ltd*

Printed in Singapore

ABOUT THE INGREDIENTS.
As seasoning is a matter of personal taste, salt and pepper are not
necessarily listed in the ingredients.
Try to obtain the best quality fresh produce.

Contents

Author's Introduction

Salmon is a fish that not only makes glorious eating but is also healthy, convenient and, nowadays, affordable. *The Salmon Cookbook* is a celebration of the worldwide availability of top-quality fresh and smoked salmon.

Historically, salmon have long been the quarry of the sportsman. Any fisherman will tell you that to stand in a river casting a line until you feel the tug of a fish on the end and then to slowly take control and land a salmon is one of the most exciting and thrilling of experiences. In fact, the amount of fish that are caught and landed this way are comparatively few. Salmon are netted in considerable quantities, both in estuaries and out at sea, but over the years demand has outstripped supply. To attempt to satisfy demand, salmon farming was conceived and put into operation. This is what brought about the revolution that has altered the status of salmon from a luxury food into a daily dish.

One of the beauties of salmon is that it can be cooked very simply, served with a pat of butter and transformed into a feast. It need not be reserved for parties or special treats and the time has come to throw aside caution and to experiment when you cook with salmon.

I feel very lucky to have been given the opportunity to write this book, and I have had a most rewarding time cooking for it and discovering just how versatile salmon is. On one hand it makes the perfect filling for a Thai omelet or it happily adapts to being served with sun-dried tomatoes in little Italian rice balls called *arancini*. After I had cooked all the international dishes featured in the book, I decided one evening to serve the simple meal of cold salmon with homemade mayonnaise, new potatoes and a good salad: It was delicious and made me realize what a truly great food salmon is.

Salmon is very easy and very quick to cook. You can poach it, broil it, fry it, cook it in the oven, on the barbecue, in the microwave or, as was a fad several years ago, wrap a whole fish in two layers of foil and put it through the hot program of the dishwasher! It will come out perfectly cooked and very moist and succulent every time.

I have tried to vary the recipes as much as possible to illustrate the amazing versatility of salmon. There are ideas here for all sorts of occasions: for quick snacks, tasty supers, picnics, barbecues, entertaining and for when you want to take a little extra trouble and produce something that will impress your partner or guests. I have also included classic salmon dishes, such as directions for cooking a whole salmon to be eaten either hot or cold and a poached salmon served with Hollandaise sauce.

In the lists of ingredients I have not named any particular species of salmon because all types can be used for any of the recipes and the method of cooking them is exactly the same. I have suggested which cut or cuts are most suitable, but if you have trouble in obtaining these, you can usually substitute a different one; you may, however, then have to alter the cooking times slightly, taking care not to overcook the salmon.

I do hope that you enjoy reading this book and, above all, cooking from it. I also hope that it might help to increase your awareness of salmon, not simply as one of the most exquisite fruits of the sea but as the most fascinating and extraordinary fish. It is truly the king of fish and the fish of kings.

Serepa Kaye

Introduction

There are eight species of salmon in all. Seven of them come from the Pacific Ocean and five of them are commonly fished or cultured, but the best-known and most widely eaten salmon is the Atlantic salmon *(Salmo Salar)*.

Fresh salmon are exported and available almost everywhere. Most of the farmed Atlantic salmon sold in the United States comes from Norway, but some is also farmed in Maine and imported from Scotland, Ireland and Canada. Wild salmon comes mainly from Alaska or along the West Coast.

The fresh fish are packed in quantities of ice in especially designed insulated boxes and flown to all corners of the world. They arrive in perfect condition, and very often within 48 hours of being caught or harvested.

All salmon are anadromous, which means that they are hatched in freshwater rivers or streams where they stay and grow until they have matured enough to enable them to live in salt water. The young salmon then migrate to the sea and remain there for one to three years. They often swim for many thousands of miles, and the Atlantic salmon that breed in Scotland, for example, are known to travel to rich feeding grounds off the coast of Greenland.

When the salmon reach maturity, they return to the freshwater to spawn, and one of the most fascinating facts is that a fish will always return to exactly the same river it was hatched in. It has not yet been discovered how the salmon are able to locate the same river and this remains one of the great mysteries of nature.

ABOVE: *A salmon farm in the picturesque Scottish Highlands.*

Farmed Salmon

Salmon used to abound in the River Thames to the extent that in the 18th-century apprentices in London went on strike until they reached an agreement that they would not be fed salmon more than three times a week. Since then, due to overfishing and pollution, stocks have diminished, but demand for salmon for the table has continued to increase. In the 1970s the serious farming of Atlantic salmon was started both in Norway and Scotland. Salmon farming has now developed into a huge, worldwide industry. Although Norway and Scotland are still by far the biggest producers, there now are farms in many other areas, notably in the cool northern waters of Maine and Canada and in the cold southern waters of Chile.

The life cycle of the farmed fish exactly mirrors that of those in the wild. Eggs from especially selected hen salmon are fertilized and hatched in special hatching trays. After a few months the fish, or fry, are transferred to pens with running freshwater or released in to the open sea. If put in a pen, they remain in it for a year, by which time they will grow to about 6 inches long and achieve the shape and color of fully grown salmon. At this stage they are known as smolts. It is at this point, about 18 months after hatching, that the smolts would naturally go to sea. The farmed ones are transferred to large pens or cages set in saltwater coastal inlets. The pens, which have nets up to 50 feet deep to give the fish ample swimming space, are positioned where there is a strong tidal flow which constantly brings in clean freshwater. As the fish grow they are divided up and moved so there is never any danger of overcrowding.

The farmers need to produce healthy fish, so for the sake of both the fish and the environment they try to avoid using chemicals and antibiotics. Unfortunately, these are occasionally needed, although they are prescribed in the minimum quantities necessary. When this occurs, the fish are kept back, tested and proved free of any trace of medication before harvesting.

Farmed salmon are fed with a carefully prepared fish meal which contains all that is needed for healthy growth. It is derived from natural food that the fish would eat in the wild and includes the essential minerals and vitamins they need, as well as the harmless substance astaxanthin, a pigment which is found naturally in wild salmon and gives them their characteristic pink color.

Some of the fish will be sold after about a year when they will weigh 2 to 4 pounds and some will be left to grow longer and sold during the following year at weights of 4 to 14 pounds. A selection of the fully grown ones will be sold and eaten as fresh fish, but many will go to the smokeries to be smoked or "pickled" and made into gravadlax, cured salmon that is eaten uncooked.

Species of Fish

Atlantic salmon

A spotted, silver skin that shines in the light and provides camouflage in the river characterizes this beautiful, lithe fish. The distinctive pink coloring of the flesh depends on a diet that is rich in shrimps. Where these are scarce, for example in the Baltic, the salmon's flesh is almost white. The Atlantic salmon is found in the rivers on the East Coast of North America and in Northern Europe, particularly Ireland, Scotland and Norway. It is widely considered to be the species that makes the best eating. Wild Atlantic salmon, now an endangered species, are netted in estuaries or caught with rod and line in rivers. A caught fish can weigh anything from 2 to 30 pounds. The record for a fish caught on rod and line was set in 1928 with a vast fish that weighed 79 pounds. Nowadays, virtually all of the Atlantic salmon sold and eaten is farmed. Its year-round availability makes it the ideal fish for a whole host of occasions. Atlantic salmon can be eaten either as a whole fish for a celebratory dinner or as steaks or fillets. Significant quantities are also smoked or cured to be eaten as gravadlax.

Pacific salmon

Pacific salmon are found all along the West Coast of the United States and Canada, and they abound in Alaska, where enormous quantities are caught in the sea and in estuaries. When the salmon return to the rivers to spawn, they arrive in vast shoals.

Chinook or King salmon. The biggest of all the salmon, with most fish weighing from 5 to 40 pounds. The mature chinook generally weighs about 20 pounds but large ones can exceed 100 pounds. The chinook, which is not as prolific in the wild as the other Pacific salmon, is now farmed off the West Coast of Canada and is available in quantity. It is known for its firm, succulent, red flesh, and it was the first salmon to be canned. Now only a few select fish are canned but many are smoked. Chinook is also popular for the table and is generally sold, fresh or frozen, in slices, steaks or fillets. Some chinook are known as white kings, due to their very light-colored flesh, and these are mainly hot smoked.

Sockeye or Red salmon. Sockeye has firm, deep-red, relatively fatty flesh. It is succulent, full of flavor and is considered one of the best species for canning. Sockeye has become popular fresh or frozen and it is also sold as steaks or fillets. The average fish weighs around 6 pounds but they can grow to 15 pounds.

Coho or Silver salmon. These fish, with their convenient size, a relatively high-fat content and a good color, are considered desirable for eating fresh and for smoking. Coho usually weigh from 2 to 12 pounds. They can be bought as whole fish, steaks or fillets.

Pink or Humpback salmon. A small salmon, this usually weighs 2 to 4 pounds. It is very common due to the fact that it arrives in large shoals. It is mostly used for canning, but is increasingly sold both fresh and frozen, usually as whole fish. Pink salmon is excellent barbecued.

Chum or Dog salmon. This salmon's firm, pink flesh is normally canned or smoked. It is available fresh or frozen, as whole fish, steaks or fillets. Usual weights are from 4 to 12 pounds for a whole fish.

Nutrition

Salmon is not only delicious to eat, but it is also one of the healthiest of foods.

Low in calories A 4-ounce serving of fresh salmon that has been broiled or baked has about 180 calories.

Protein The fish is an excellent source of high-quality protein and contains all the essential amino acids.

Low cholesterol Salmon is an oily fish, but the fats it contains are largely unsaturated, and it is rich in omega-3 or long-chain polyunsaturates. There is evidence that intake of these omega-3 polyunsaturated fatty acids can help to avoid the development of artery and heart diseases. They are frequently recommended following heart surgery, to aid the reduction of high blood pressure and they can also give relief to sufferers of arthritis, inflamation of the joints and eczema.

Good source of vitamins Salmon contains vitamins A, D, B_6 (pyridoxine) and B_{12} (cobalamin), as well as niacin and riboflavin.

Mineral content. High in minerals, including calcium, iron, zinc, magnesium and phosphorus.

Buying and Storing Salmon

Always buy salmon which is as fresh as possible. Check for freshness by making sure that the flesh is firm to the touch, the gills are red or pink and the skin bright and shiny. Do not, for example, buy any fillets or steaks that are starting to turn yellow or brown around the edges. Another significant key to a salmon's freshness is its smell. A fresh salmon will only have a very mild smell. If it has a "fishy" smell, it is probably several days old or has not been properly stored and should not be purchased.

Store salmon either in its package or loosely wrapped in foil in the refrigerator. Consume it as soon as possible and always by the date given on the packaging.

Frozen salmon should not be kept for any more than a month and should be slowly defrosted to room temperature before cooking. If you are buying fish that has been frozen and thawed, ask the fish merchant or sales assistant how long it has been thawed. Do not buy the fish if it has been thawed for more than two days.

Using your Microwave

Salmon's oily flesh lends itself to a variety of quick cooking techniques such as poaching, baking, broiling, frying and barbecuing, and can be cooked very successfully in the microwave.

A microwave is extremely useful for cooking salmon. It makes poaching quick and easy and cooked salmon can be ready in minutes when it is needed for a recipe. A tail piece can be cooked in the microwave but do not attempt to cook a whole fish or a center cut; they are both too thick and solid and will not cook right through.

Timings are listed on page 12 as a guide for cooking salmon in the microwave. Let the fish stand for 1 to 2 minutes after you remove it from the microwave so it cooks through to the center. To ensure the fish is cooked through, use a fork to separate the flesh slightly, and if it is still at all raw return it to the microwave for 30 seconds longer.

The timings given are for a 650-watt microwave and are for two steaks or pieces of fillet. For one piece, cut about one-third from the time, and for four pieces add another 50 percent. Also add or subtract time if the pieces of fish are bigger or smaller than the examples given. Pieces that are over 1 inch thick may cook more evenly if turned half way through the cooking time.

The best way of cooking the fish is to arrange it like the spokes of a wheel in a shallow microwave-safe dish with the thickest part at the outside edge. Dot with a little butter or sprinkle with 1 tablespoon of water, wine or milk. Partially cover the dish with a lid or stretch a piece of microwave-safe plastic wrap over it and pierce several times with a knife.

BELOW: Salmon steaks, fillet and a tail piece.

• 2 x 6- to 7-ounce salmon steaks will take $4^{1}/_{2}$ minutes on High (100%).

• 2 x 5- to 6-ounce pieces of salmon fillet will take $3^{1}/_{2}$ minutes on High (100%). Smaller steaks or pieces of fillet are best cooked for the same time on 80% (Medium-High) power.

• 1 x 1-pound tail piece will take 5 minutes on High (100%).

• If you need cooked salmon for a recipe and do not have any left over fish, you can quickly place a steak or fillet in the microwave. Sprinkle 1 tablespoon water over the fish. In a 650-watt oven, microwave on 80% power (Medium-High), turning the fish half way through, for $3^{1}/_{2}$ minutes. For two pieces of steak or fillet, increase the cooking time to $4^{1}/_{2}$ to $5^{1}/_{2}$ minutes.

• Salmon can also be thawed in the microwave. In a 650-watt oven, put the frozen steak or fillet into a dish, cover and cook on 80% power (Medium-High), turning once, for 2 minutes longer. Leave to stand for 2 minutes longer and then check to ensure that the fish is completely thawed.

Hints and Tips

When buying salmon ask the fish merchant if it has been frozen and, if so, do not freeze it again before cooking.

• Fish merchants often sell tail pieces of salmon at a good price. The flesh is very sweet and tender and this cut is well worth buying. Cut small fillets from a tail piece or cook it whole, either by poaching or baking in foil in the oven. A tail piece of salmon is also a very good buy when you need flaked fish for a recipe.

• Before cooking a whole salmon remove any stray scales or bones by washing it under cold water. Pat it dry, both inside and out, with paper towels.

• Never wash steaks, fillets or pieces of cut salmon as the juices from the fish will drain away. Clean by patting the fish all over with a piece of damp paper towel.

• One 6-ounce salmon steak will, after cooking and discarding the skin and bone, yield approximately $3^{1}/_{2}$ ounces flaked salmon

• Salmon can be cooked on the stovetop, in the oven, under the broiler, in the microwave, or on a barbecue.

• Baking salmon in foil in its own juices preserves the flavor and nutrients to the full. It is just as easy to bake a whole fish as it is to bake several steaks.

• Be careful not to overcook salmon because the flesh will separate and taste chewy. A good rule of thumb is to cook it for slightly less time than you think is needed. Remember that it will continue to cook for a minute or so after removing it from the heat.

• When broiling salmon steaks choose thick ones — thin ones dry out quickly.

• Spread a little melted butter onto salmon steaks or fillets about 20 minutes before broiling them. The butter will soak in and keep the flesh succulent and moist. Or sprinkle some salt over the fish about 2 minutes before putting it under the broiler. The salt will draw out the natural juices which will stop the outside of the salmon from becoming dry.

• Flake salmon soon after cooking, while it is still warm.

• Before cutting cooled cooked salmon into slices or strips, refrigerate it for several hours or put it in the freezer for a short time. The cut flesh will then hold its shape.

• For smoked salmon recipes that use either chopped or strips of smoked salmon you can buy offcuts, which are very economical. Ask for slightly more than the recipe specifies because they will need picking over and any hard edges or brown pieces removed.

RIGHT: Fish poacher and whole salmon.

Soups and Appetizers

A hearty chowder for a family supper, a delicate soup flavored with coconut milk or salmon pâté with whole-wheat toast; a range of first courses can be produced using salmon, making the most of its attractive color and texture.

Salmon and Corn Chowder

2 tablespoons BUTTER
1 MEDIUM CARROT, DICED
1 SMALL ONION, CHOPPED
white part of 1 LEEK, CHOPPED
1 medium POTATO, PEELED AND CUBED
2 1/2 cups MILK
SALT AND PEPPER
1 x 7-ounce can CORN, DRAINED
6 ounces SALMON FILLET, SKINNED AND CUBED
2/3 cup HEAVY CREAM
1 tablespoon CHOPPED FRESH PARSLEY

Melt the butter in a pan. Add the carrot and cook for 2 minutes. Add the onion and leek and stir until transparent. Stir in the potato and cook for 1 minute longer before pouring in the milk and 1 1/4 cups water. Season well and heat to just below boiling point, then simmer gently for 10 minutes. Add the corn and the salmon and simmer for another 3-4 minutes. Stir in the cream and the parsley. Spoon into heated bowls and serve immediately. SERVES 4-6

Coconut Milk and Salmon Soup

3 3/4 cups LIGHT CHICKEN OR VEGETABLE STOCK
1 STALK FRESH LEMONGRASS, CHOPPED
1/2-inch PIECE FRESH GINGER ROOT, PEELED AND CHOPPED
grated zest of 1 LEMON
1/2 DRIED RED CHILI
6 ounces SALMON FILLET, SKINNED
1 tablespoon CORNSTARCH
1 tablespoon LEMON JUICE
1 x 12-ounce CAN COCONUT MILK
SALT AND PEPPER
small bunch CILANTRO, CHOPPED

Put the stock in a pan with the lemongrass, ginger, lemon zest and chili. Bring to a boil, then simmer for 10 minutes. Strain. Purée the salmon in a blender or food processor. Pour a cupful of the stock through the feed tube, then add the mixture to the rinsed-out pan along with the rest of the stock. Mix the cornstarch and lemon juice together and add them to the pan along with the coconut milk. Season to taste. Cook, stirring over medium heat until the soup thickens. Sprinkle with the cilantro and serve. SERVES 4

TOP: Salmon and Corn Chowder
BOTTOM: Coconut Milk and Salmon Soup

Chilled Salmon Soup

1 x 6 1/8-ounce CAN PINK SALMON
2 x 15-ounce CANS VICHYSSOISE SOUP
2/3 cup SOUR CREAM
1 bunch CHIVES, SNIPPED

Purée the salmon and one can of the vichyssoise in a blender or food processor. Pour the purée into a bowl, then stir in the remaining can of vichyssoise. Refrigerate for at least 1 hour.

Ladle the soup into bowls, swirl a little sour cream into each bowl and serve with the snipped chives sprinkled over the top. SERVES 4

Watercress and Salmon Roulade with Red Pepper Sauce

Red Pepper Sauce
2 RED BELL PEPPERS, SEEDED AND QUARTERED
grated zest and juice of 1 ORANGE
SALT AND PEPPER

Roulade
1 cup FRESH WHITE BREAD CRUMBS
1/4 cup FRESHLY GRATED PARMESAN CHEESE
2/3 cup CHOPPED WATERCRESS
4 EGGS, SEPARATED
2/3 cup LIGHT CREAM

Filling
8 ounces SALMON, POACHED, BONED, SKINNED AND FLAKED
3 tablespoons MAYONNAISE
1 tablespoon FRESHLY GRATED PARMESAN CHEESE

To make the sauce, broil the peppers, skin sides up, until they are black and charred. Put into a plastic bag. Cool. Peel off the skins, roughly chop the flesh and purée in a blender or food processor. Transfer to a bowl and stir in the orange zest and juice. Season to taste.

To make the roulade, line a 13-inch x 9-inch jelly-roll pan with a piece of parchment paper and preheat the oven to 400°F.

Combine the bread crumbs, Parmesan and watercress, then stir in the egg yolks and cream. Season to taste. Beat the egg whites until stiff, then fold into the mixture. Spoon into the prepared pan, level the surface and bake for 12 – 14 minutes or until the center is firm. Remove from the oven and cover with a damp dish towel.

Meanwhile, mix the salmon and mayonnaise together and season to taste. Sprinkle the Parmesan over a sheet of wax paper and invert the roulade onto it. Spread the filling over the roulade and roll it up from the long side. Wrap the wax paper around it and refrigerate. Remove the paper before serving. Slice the roulade and serve accompanied by the sauce. SERVES 6-8

RIGHT: Watercress and Salmon Roulade with Red Pepper Sauce

Spinach and Salmon Custards

Six rounded molds, or cups that have been well greased with butter, are needed for this recipe.

3 EGGS
1 1/4 cups LIGHT CREAM
6 ounces FROZEN CHOPPED SPINACH, DEFROSTED
4 ounces SALMON, POACHED AND FLAKED
pinch GRATED NUTMEG
SALT AND PEPPER
BUTTER FOR GREASING
FRESHLY GRATED PARMESAN CHEESE

Preheat the oven to 350°F. Lightly beat the eggs and cream together. Stir in the spinach and salmon. Season with nutmeg and salt and pepper.

Divide the mixture between the prepared molds and place them in a water bath in the oven. Bake for 25 minutes or until set.

Turn out the custards and serve hot sprinkled with Parmesan cheese. SERVES 6

Mousseline with Fresh Tomato Sauce

A blender or food processor is essential to make a featherlight mousseline. Keep everything refrigerated and very cold. Even the food processor bowl can be chilled in the freezer for 20 minutes before using.

10 ounces SALMON FILLET, SKINNED AND CUBED
1 CLOVE GARLIC, CHOPPED
1 EGG
1 EXTRA EGG WHITE
SALT AND PEPPER
1 1/4 cups HEAVY CREAM
1 sprig DILL, TO GARNISH

Fresh Tomato Sauce
2 1/2 cups SKINNED, SEEDED AND FINELY
CHOPPED TOMATOES
2/3 cup LIGHT CREAM
2 teaspoons LEMON JUICE
1 teaspoon SUGAR
1 tablespoon CHOPPED DILL

Purée the salmon and garlic in a blender or food processor for about 2 minutes. Add the egg and the extra egg white. Season. Turn the processor on again to mix them, then, with it still running, add the very cold cream through the feed tube. Stop as soon as the mixture is thick and smooth. Chill.

Preheat the oven to 350°F and put a roasting pan half-full of very hot water into it. Generously grease a 2 1/2-cup terrine or bread pan. Spoon in the mousseline mixture and cover with a piece of greased foil. Put in the water bath and bake for 30-35 minutes or until the top is firm. Cool.

Meanwhile, make the sauce by combining the tomatoes with all the other ingredients. Turn the mousseline out onto a dish and slice. Serve garnished with the dill and accompanied by the sauce. SERVES 6

TOP: Spinach and Salmon Custards
BOTTOM: Mousseline with Tomato Sauce

Stuffed Thai Omelets

The filling for these omelets is flavored with the Thai fish sauce, nam pla. *If this is not available, substitute lemon juice.*

2 tablespoons OIL

3 SCALLIONS, CHOPPED (RESERVE THE GREEN PARTS FOR GARNISH)

1 CLOVE GARLIC, FINELY CHOPPED

1/2 teaspoon FINELY CHOPPED FRESH GINGER ROOT

5 ounces SALMON FILLET, SKINNED AND CUT INTO 1/2-INCH CUBES

3 ounces BEAN SPROUTS

2 teaspoons SOY SAUCE

1 tablespoon NAM PLA FISH SAUCE

2 tablespoons SWEET SHERRY COMBINED WITH 1 teaspoon CORNSTARCH

SALT AND FRESHLY GROUND PEPPER

3 EGGS

2 tablespoons BUTTER

Heat 1 tablespoon of the oil and gently fry the white part of the scallions, the garlic and the ginger. When the onions are transparent, add the salmon cubes and stir constantly for 1 minute or until they are just cooked. Use a slotted spoon to remove the contents of the pan and set aside. Add another spoonful of oil to the pan and cook the bean sprouts, stirring, for 1 minute or until they have wilted. Sprinkle in the soy sauce and *nam pla*, then stir in the sherry and cornstarch mixture and a good grinding of pepper. Bring to a boil and let it thicken. Return the salmon to the pan and mix it in. Keep warm.

To make 6 omelets, beat the eggs, adding 2 tablespoons cold water and salt and pepper. Melt a knob of butter with a dribble of oil in a 6-inch skillet. When it is hot, pour in a little of the egg mixture and swirl it around to cover the bottom of the pan. Cook until set, then slide onto a warm plate. Cover and keep warm. Make another 5 omelets in the same way.

Divide the filling between the omelets. Fold in the sides so that they overlap and resemble square pillows. Transfer to a plate with the folds underneath. Garnish with a little of the green from the scallions.   SERVES 6

Salmon and Turbot Seviche

12 ounces SALMON FILLET, SKINNED

8 ounces TURBOT FILLET, SKINNED

juice of 2 LIMES

4 tablespoons OLIVE OIL

To Garnish

1 bunch CHIVES, SNIPPED

LOLLO ROSSO LETTUCE LEAVES

2/3 cup SLICED BUTTON MUSHROOMS

Cut the fish into thin strips, then arrange in rows on 4 plates. Brush the fish with the lime juice and leave to marinate or "cook" for 30 minutes. Drizzle the olive oil over the fish, garnish and serve.   SERVES 4

RIGHT: Stuffed Thai Omelets

Salmon and Herb Pâté

1 1/4 pounds TAIL PIECE OF SALMON

2/3 cup WHITE WINE

1 SMALL ONION, CHOPPED

2 BAY LEAVES

1 BUNCH PARSLEY STEMS

1 ENVELOPE UNFLAVORED GELATIN

2 teaspoons LIME JUICE

3 tablespoons CHOPPED PARSLEY

2 tablespoons EACH OF SORREL AND CHERVIL

2 tablespoons SNIPPED CHIVES

SALT AND PEPPER

Sauce

2/3 cup MAYONNAISE

2/3 cup PLAIN YOGURT

grated zest of 1 LEMON

1 teaspoon TOMATO PASTE

1 teaspoon CAPERS, DRAINED

Put the salmon into a pan with the wine, onion, bay leaves, parsley stems and enough water to just cover the fish. Bring to a boil, then simmer for 10 minutes. Remove the salmon from the pan, reheat the stock and boil fast until it has reduced to about 1 1/4 cups. Strain and leave to cool. Transfer 2 tablespoons stock to a small bowl. Sprinkle the gelatin over and melt it by placing the bowl over a pan of simmering water. Stir it into the stock, then add the lime juice and keep warm.

Skin and bone the salmon and divide it into flakes. Place in a bowl and stir in two-thirds of the stock and the herbs. Season to taste. Spoon into a greased terrine or bowl. Refrigerate until set, then spoon the remaining stock over and chill again until set.

To make the sauce, mix all the ingredients together.

Serve the pâté accompanied by a bowl of the sauce and whole-wheat toast. SERVES 6

Rillettes

The combination of fresh and smoked salmon has a texture similar to rillettes, a French pâté.

4 tablespoons UNSALTED BUTTER, SOFTENED

grated zest and juice of 1/2 LEMON

2 SPRIGS THYME, CHOPPED

SALT AND PEPPER

pinch CAYENNE PEPPER

4 ounces SALMON, POACHED, SKINNED, BONED AND FLAKED

2 ounces SMOKED SALMON, CHOPPED

1 sprig CHERVIL, TO GARNISH

Combine the butter with the lemon zest and juice and the thyme. Season with salt, pepper and cayenne to taste. Mash in the cooked salmon – do not make it too smooth – and finally the smoked salmon.

Garnish, and serve with bread or toast, or as a dip with potato chips or tortilla chips. SERVES 4

TOP: Salmon and Herb Pâté

BOTTOM: Rillettes

Lemon Sole and Salmon Terrine

Look in delicatessens and gourmet food stores for packages of imported aspic powder, often described as aspic jelly on the envelope. This is dissolved to make the thick, clear gelatin used to coat this terrine. If you can not find aspic powder, dissolve 1 tablespoon unflavored gelatin in 1 1/2 cups fish stock. Be sure to use a very clear stock or your aspic will be cloudy.

1 pound	SALMON FILLET, SKINNED, POACHED AND CHILLED
4	LEMON SOLE FILLETS, SKINNED, COOKED AND CHILLED
2	RED BELL PEPPERS, SEEDED AND QUARTERED
1	BUNCH PARSLEY
1	LEMON
1	ENVELOPE ASPIC POWDER
1	HARD-BOILED EGG, SLICED

To Garnish
ARUGULA
CHERRY TOMATOES, PEELED

Cut both chilled fish into thin strips and set aside.

Broil the peppers, skin sides up, until the skins are charred and cracked. Put the hot pepper quarters into a plastic bag, seal well and leave for 20 minutes. Peel off the skins and cut the flesh into strips. Reserve a few parsley sprigs and chop the remainder.

Peel the lemon using a sharp knife. Remove as much pith as possible from the peel and blanch the peel in boiling water for 2 minutes. Drain and cut the peel into attractive shapes. Set aside.

Generously grease a 9- x 5- x 3-inch bread pan. Make up the aspic powder following the directions on the package. To stop it from setting, keep it in the bowl over a pan of warm water.

Pour a very thin layer of aspic into the pan and refrigerate, or put in the freezer, until set. Arrange the hard-boiled egg slices, some parsley sprigs, lemon peel and a few pieces of pepper (both skin sides down) on the set aspic. Cover with a little more aspic and leave to set.

Make another layer with the salmon, lemon sole, pepper strips and chopped parsley. Continue making layers with a little aspic, allowing it to set before starting on the next one. Cover and refrigerate. Discard any left-over aspic.

To serve, briefly immerse the bottom of the pan in very hot water. Run a knife around the inside, then unmold onto a plate. Garnish with parsley.   SERVES 6-8

RIGHT: Lemon Sole and Salmon Terrine

Spanish-style Fritters

These fritters are based on buñueles, *a delicious snack found in tapas bars throughout Spain.*

EXTRA VEGETABLE OIL FOR FRYING
LEMON WEDGES FOR SERVING

Batter
1 EGG
1 cup ALL-PURPOSE FLOUR
1/2 teaspoon BAKING POWDER
1/2 teaspoon SALT

Filling
1 tablespoon VEGETABLE OIL
1 SMALL ONION, CHOPPED
8 ounces SALMON, CHOPPED
2 tablespoons CHOPPED PARSLEY
SALT AND PEPPER

In a small measuring jug, lightly beat the egg and 1/2 cup water together in a bowl. Stir the flour, baking powder and salt together in a bowl, then slowly add the egg-and-water mixture. Set aside.

Heat the 1 tablespoon oil. Sauté the onion until transparent, then stir it into the salmon. Add the parsley and season to taste. Pour in the batter and stir. Pour some more oil to a depth of 1/2 inch into a skillet and heat. Drop tablespoonsful of the salmon batter into the medium-hot oil and cook for 2-3 minutes on each side or until brown. Drain on paper towels. Keep warm in the oven while frying the remainder. Serve immediately with lemon wedges. MAKES 10-20 FRITTERS

Creamy Croustades

8 SLICES BREAD
OLIVE OIL
6 ounces CREAM CHEESE
6 ounces SALMON, COOKED, SKINNED AND FLAKED
2 tablespoons SLIVERED ALMONDS, TOASTED
1 teaspoon PAPRIKA
FLAT-LEAF PARSLEY, TO GARNISH

Preheat the oven to 400°F. Cut the crusts from the bread and discard. Roll the bread slices with a rolling pin until they are very thin. Cut out a circle from each slice using a 3-inch cutter. Brush both sides of the circles with a little olive oil, then press them into muffin pan molds or tartlet pans. Bake for 5-10 minutes.

Mash the cream cheese, then stir in the salmon and the nuts and season to taste. Spoon into the prepared croustades, sprinkle a little paprika on each one and garnish. SERVES 4

TOP: Spanish-Style Fritters
BOTTOM: Creamy Croustades

Salads

Salmon can be cooked in advance and cooled in preparation for salads with rice or pasta or for adding to green salads. It can be added to mousses and tarts for summer meals or first courses. The vinaigrettes and sauces in these recipes are for tossing or serving separately.

Salmon and Shrimp Salad

Mayonnaise
2 EGG YOLKS
1 tablespoon FRESH ORANGE JUICE
1 tablespoon SUNFLOWER OIL
1 tablespoon OLIVE OIL
grated zest of 1 ORANGE

Salad
1 head CRISP GREEN LETTUCE, SHREDDED
1 head LOLLO ROSSO LETTUCE OR
RADICCHIO, SHREDDED
1 pound SALMON, POACHED, SKINNED,
BONED AND CUBED
12 ounces SHRIMP, DEFROSTED
3 cups HALVED BUTTON MUSHROOMS
2 tablespoons PINE NUTS, TOASTED

Make the mayonnaise following the directions on page 66, but use orange juice in place of vinegar.

Divide the lettuces between 4 serving glasses or bowls. Mix the salmon, shrimp, mushrooms and mayonnaise together. Divide between the bowls and sprinkle with pine nuts.   SERVES 6

Stuffed Cherry Tomatoes

8 ounces CHERRY TOMATOES
5 ounces SALMON, POACHED, SKINNED AND BONED
5 tablespoons MAYONNAISE
1 tablespoon PESTO SAUCE
DRESSED LETTUCE LEAVES
SPRIG BASIL, TO GARNISH

Cut the tops off the tomatoes and reserve. Spoon out the flesh. Flake the salmon. Combine the mayonnaise and pesto sauce, then fold in the salmon. Season to taste. Spoon into the tomato shells and use the tomato tops as lids; there may be some filling left over.

Arrange the tomatoes on a few lightly-dressed lettuce leaves and garnish with a sprig of basil.   SERVES 4

TOP: Salmon and Shrimp Salad
BOTTOM: Stuffed Cherry Tomatoes

Salad Bowl

2 tablespoons VEGETABLE OIL
1 CLOVE GARLIC, CRUSHED
2 SLICES BREAD, WITH CRUSTS REMOVED,
CUBED
3 tablespoons FRESHLY GRATED PARMESAN CHEESE
1 head CRISP LETTUCE, SHREDDED
handful MÂCHE
1 small bunch RADISHES, SLICED
1 AVOCADO, CUBED
4 ears BABY CORN, SLICED
12 ounces to 1 pound SALMON, POACHED, BONED, SKINNED
AND CUBED

Vinaigrette
1 CLOVE GARLIC
SALT AND FRESHLY GROUND BLACK PEPPER
2 teaspoons WINE VINEGAR
3 tablespoons OLIVE OIL

Heat the oil and gently cook the garlic. Fry the bread cubes, adding more oil if necessary, until brown and crisp. Drain the croutons on paper towels, then mix with 2 tablespoons of the cheese. Assemble all the other ingredients in a large salad bowl.

To make the vinaigrette, crush the garlic with salt, add freshly ground black pepper and stir in the vinegar. Add the oil and whisk. Pour the dressing over the salad and toss gently. Finally, sprinkle on the remaining Parmesan and the croutons. Serve immediately.   SERVES 4

Mixed Bean and Fish Salad

6 ounces FRENCH-STYLE GREEN BEANS
SALT
1 x 14 1/2 ounce CAN FLAGEOLET OR NAVY BEANS
1 RED ONION, HALVED AND THINLY SLICED
1 tablespoon CHOPPED OREGANO
2 tablespoons CHOPPED PARSLEY
8 ounces SALMON FILLET, POACHED AND CHILLED
8 ounces MONKFISH, POACHED AND CHILLED
3 tablespoons OLIVE OIL
2 tablespoons BALSAMIC VINEGAR
1 CLOVE GARLIC, CRUSHED

Top, tail and halve the beans. Cook for 3 minutes in a pan of boiling salted water. Drain. Rinse under cold water and drain again. Drain and rinse the flageolet or navy beans. Put the green beans, flageolet or navy beans, onion slices and herbs into a salad bowl. Skin the salmon and monkfish, then cut into bite-size pieces. Carefully stir into the bowl.

Whisk the olive oil, vinegar and garlic together and pour over the salad. Toss gently. Chill until ready to serve.   SERVES 4

TOP: *Salad Bowl*

BOTTOM: *Mixed Bean and Fish Salad*

Paprika-Rice Salad

3/4 cup LONG-GRAIN RICE

1 RED BELL PEPPER, SEEDED AND QUARTERED

1 tablespoon VEGETABLE OIL

1 SMALL ONION, CHOPPED

2 CLOVES GARLIC, CRUSHED

1 teaspoon PAPRIKA

2 teaspoons TOMATO PASTE

juice of 1 LEMON

4 tablespoons PLAIN YOGURT

2/3 cup MAYONNAISE

1 head CRISP LETTUCE

4 x 4- to 5-ounce PIECES SALMON FILLET, POACHED AND CHILLED

Cook the rice as directed on the package. Finely chop three-quarters of the pepper. Heat the oil in a skillet and sauté the onion and garlic until soft. Add the paprika and tomato paste and cook, stirring, for 1 minute, then add the lemon juice and 3 tablespoons water. Bring to a boil, then simmer for 2 minutes. Remove from the heat and stir into the rice.

Roughly chop the remaining pepper. Purée in a blender or food processor. Add the yogurt and blend together. Stir the pepper and yogurt into the mayonnaise and season to taste.

Shred the lettuce and arrange it in the center of a large serving dish. Spoon the salmon onto the bed of lettuce and surround it with the rice. Pour the sauce over the fish.   SERVES 4

Colorful Pasta Salad

6 ounces PASTA SHAPES

8 ounces ASPARAGUS

SALT AND PEPPER

4 tablespoons OLIVE OIL

1 teaspoon WHITE-WINE VINEGAR

grated zest and juice of 1/2 LEMON

2 tablespoons CHOPPED CHERVIL OR PARSLEY

6 ounces SALMON, POACHED, SKINNED, BONED AND DIVIDED INTO LARGE FLAKES

1 tablespoon FRESHLY GRATED PARMESAN CHEESE

Cook the pasta as directed on the package. Drain and rinse well, then set aside.

Trim the asparagus. Remove and reserve the heads and cut the stalks at an angle into 1½-inch pieces. Bring a pan of salted water to a boil. Add the stalks and cook for 3 minutes or until tender. Remove with a slotted spoon. Add the asparagus heads to the pan and cook for 2 minutes. Drain and set aside.

To make the dressing, beat the oil, vinegar and lemon juice together. Stir in half the herbs and the lemon zest. Season to taste.

Toss the pasta in the dressing. Add the asparagus stalks and salmon and toss gently. Transfer to a serving dish. Arrange the asparagus heads on top and sprinkle the remaining herbs and the Parmesan over.   SERVES 4

TOP: *Paprika-Rice Salad*
BOTTOM: *Colorful Pasta Salad*

Salmon and Cucumber Tart

1/4 cup WHITE WINE

2 teaspoons UNFLAVORED GELATIN

7 tablespoons PLAIN YOGURT

7 tablespoons MAYONNAISE

SALT AND PEPPER

1 tablespoon FINELY CHOPPED DILL OR

1/2 teaspoon DRIED DILL WEED

8 ounces SALMON, POACHED, SKINNED, BONED AND FLAKED

1/2 CUCUMBER, PEELED, SEEDED AND CUBED

1 x 7-inch BAKED PASTRY SHELL

LETTUCE LEAVES AND CUCUMBER SLICES, TO GARNISH

Pour the wine into a small bowl and sprinkle in the gelatin. Place the bowl over a pan of simmering water to dissolve the gelatin.

In a larger bowl, combine the yogurt and mayonnaise. Season well, then stir in the dill, wine, and gelatin. Add the salmon and cucumber and mix together well. Spoon into the pastry shell, level the surface and leave to set. Garnish with lettuce leaves and slices of cucumber.

SERVES 4

Salmon Mousse

1 x 6 1/8-ounce CAN RED SALMON, DRAINED, BONED AND FLAKED

2/3 cup LIGHT CREAM

1 EGG, SEPARATED

1 ENVELOPE UNFLAVORED GELATIN

2 tablespoons WINE VINEGAR

2/3 cup MAYONNAISE

1/3 cup FINELY CHOPPED PITTED GREEN OLIVES

1/2 teaspoon GREEN PEPPERCORNS

white part of 1 SCALLION, FINELY CHOPPED

grated zest and juice of 1/2 LEMON

Mash the salmon with a fork and set aside.

In a small pan, heat the cream to near boiling point. Beat the egg yolk with a fork, then pour the hot cream onto it. Return to the pan over very gentle heat and stir constantly until the mixture thickens. Remove from the heat, pour into a bowl and leave to cool.

Dissolve the gelatin, following the directions on the package, in 2 tablespoons water, then stir it into the cooled cream. Stir in the salmon, vinegar, mayonnaise, olives, peppercorns, scallion, and lemon zest and juice. Stir together well, then season to taste. Leave until it is just about to set, then quickly beat the egg white until stiff and fold it in. Pour the mixture into a greased 3 3/4-cup mold. Refrigerate until set. Unmold onto a plate and serve.

SERVES 4-6

RIGHT: Salmon and Cucumber Tart

Main Courses

Pan-fried, baked, broiled or poached *en papillote,* salmon makes a superb focal point for a meal. Steaks and fillets both cook very quickly, their flavors enhanced by the addition of a sprinkling of herbs or a tasty marinade.

Salmon Steaks with Hollandaise Sauce

4 SALMON STEAKS

Hollandaise Sauce
2 tablespoons LEMON JUICE
4 BLACK PEPPERCORNS
3 EGG YOLKS
3/4 cup BUTTER, CUBED
SALT AND PEPPER

Court Bouillon
1 1/4 cups WHITE WINE OR
6 tablespoons WHITE-WINE VINEGAR OR
juice of 1 LEMON MADE UP TO 1 1/4 CUPS WITH
    WATER
1 ONION, SLICED
1 SMALL CARROT, SLICED
1 STALK CELERY, CHOPPED
BOUQUET GARNI

To Garnish
1 sprig PARSLEY
LEMON SLICES

First make the sauce. Put the lemon juice, peppercorns and 2 tablespoons water into a small pan. Boil to reduce to 1 tablespoon liquid. Put the egg yolks into a bowl. Strain the reduced liquid over them, then place the bowl over a pan of just-simmering water. Beat the mixture together, then beat in the butter, cube by cube, beating constantly. Keep the sauce warm, but not hot, and if it overheats and starts to separate, remove the bowl from the pan and plunge the bottom into a bowl of cold water. Beat until the sauce is smooth, then return the bowl to the pan and continue. When all the butter has been amalgamated, season to taste.

To make the court bouillon, put all the ingredients into a large sauté pan or saucepan and add 3 3/4 cups water. Bring to a boil, then simmer for 20 minutes. Strain and return to the pan. Add the salmon steaks. Simmer gently for 5 minutes, or longer if they are thick steaks or need turning because they are not covered by the court bouillon. Check that they are cooked through by inserting a fork to see if the bone comes away from the flesh.

Remove the salmon steaks with a slotted spoon, and drain well. Garnish with a sprig of parsley and lemon slices. Serve immediately with the sauce.   SERVES 4

RIGHT: Salmon Steaks with Hollandaise Sauce

Oven-Baked Salmon with Garlic and Lentils

Lentils

1 tablespoon OLIVE OIL
grated zest and juice of 1 ORANGE
SALT AND PEPPER
1 cup GREEN LENTILS
1 SMALL ONION STUCK WITH 1 CLOVE
1 BOUQUET GARNI

Salmon

2 tablespoons OLIVE OIL
2 CLOVES GARLIC, CHOPPED
2 tablespoons CHOPPED PARSLEY
grated zest of 1 ORANGE
4 SALMON STEAKS

To make the dressing for the lentils, beat the oil and orange juice together, then stir in the zest, season well and set aside.

Put the lentils, onion and bouquet garni into a pan. Cover with water and bring to a boil, then simmer for 45 minutes or until the lentils are tender. Drain. Discard the onion and bouquet garni. Stir the oil and orange juice mixture into the lentils. Keep warm.

Meanwhile, preheat the oven to 350°F. To prepare the salmon, pour the oil into a baking dish. Stir in the garlic, then cover and put in the oven for 10 minutes or until the oil is sizzling. Sprinkle with the parsley and orange zest. Add the salmon steaks, turning them over to coat with oil. Cover and return to the oven for 8-10 minutes or until the salmon is just cooked and a knife will slide in easily next to the bone.

Transfer the lentils to a serving dish. Top with the salmon steaks and pour the garlic-flavored juices over them. SERVES 4

Broiled Salmon with Teriyaki Sauce

The slightly sweet Japanese sauce complements salmon perfectly.

3 tablespoons SOY SAUCE
4 tablespoons RICE WINE OR SWEET SHERRY
1 tablespoon SUGAR
1 teaspoon PEELED AND FINELY CHOPPED FRESH
GINGER ROOT
4 SALMON STEAKS

Combine the first four ingredients in a small saucepan. Cook until slightly reduced and syrupy. Brush the steaks lightly with the sauce and set aside for 20 minutes.

Preheat the broiler. Put the steaks on the broiler rack. Brush on a little more of the sauce and broil, not too close to the heat, for 4 minutes. Turn the fish over, brush again with the sauce and broil for 3-4 minutes longer or until a knife will slide in easily next to the bone. Serve with any remaining sauce poured over the steaks. SERVES 4

RIGHT: Oven-Baked Salmon with Garlic and Lentils

Salmon with Orange and Mustard Sauce

the white part of 3 SCALLIONS, CHOPPED
grated zest and juice of 1 LARGE ORANGE
PEPPER
4 x 5-ounce SALMON STEAKS
4 tablespoons BUTTER
1 tablespoon DIJON MUSTARD
2/3 cup LIGHT CREAM
1 teaspoon LEMON JUICE
SALT

To Garnish
1 sprig PARSLEY
ORANGE SLICES

Put the scallions, orange zest and juice and a good grinding of pepper on a flat dish that is big enough to hold the salmon steaks in a single layer. Turn the salmon steaks in the marinade and leave for about 45 minutes, turning once or twice.

Melt the butter and heat to sizzling point in a skillet. Scrape the marinade pieces from the salmon back into the dish. Fry the salmon for 3-4 minutes each side or slightly longer if the steaks are thick until a knife slides in easily next to the bone. Remove the fish from the pan and keep warm.

Add the marinade to the pan and bring to a boil. Boil for 1 minute, then stir in the mustard, cream and lemon juice. Season with salt. Let it bubble up, then simmer for a further minute. Remove the pan from the heat, add the butter and stir it in. Pour the sauce over the salmon steaks, garnish and serve immediately. SERVES 4

Piquant Pan-Fried Salmon

2 tablespoons OLIVE OIL
4 SALMON STEAKS
4 tablespoons BUTTER
2 tablespoons CAPERS, DRAINED AND RINSED
2 tablespoons WHITE-WINE VINEGAR
SALT AND PEPPER
1 tablespoon CHOPPED PARSLEY

Heat the oil in a skillet. Add the salmon and fry for 1 minute each side. Reduce the heat and cook for a further 3-5 minutes on each side or until a fork will slide in easily next to the bone. Transfer the salmon to a dish, cover and keep warm.

Melt the butter in the skillet. Add the vinegar and capers and bring to a boil, then simmer for 2 minutes, stirring occasionally. Remove from the heat, season to taste and stir in the parsley. Pour the sauce over the salmon steaks. SERVES 4

TOP: Salmon with Orange and Mustard Sauce
BOTTOM: Piquant Pan-Fried Salmon

Salmon in Fruit and Nut Sauce

4 tablespoons BUTTER
4 SALMON STEAKS
5 ounces MUSCAT GRAPES
grated zest and juice of 1/2 LIME
2 tablespoons ALMONDS, TOASTED
SALT AND PEPPER

To Garnish
FRESH CILANTRO
LIME WEDGES

Melt the butter in a skillet. Add the salmon steaks and cook for 1 minute each side. Reduce the heat and cook for a further 3-5 minutes on each side or until a knife will slide in easily next to the bone, depending on the thickness. Remove from the skillet and keep warm.

Peel and halve the grapes, then remove the seeds. Stir the lime zest and juice into the pan. Add the grapes and cook gently for 2 minutes. Stir in the almonds. Season to taste. Cook for a further minute. Pour the sauce over the salmon steaks, garnish and serve.   SERVES 4

Baked Salmon with a Brioche Crust

1 x 3-ounce SLICE FROM A BRIOCHE LOAF
1 SHALLOT, FINELY CHOPPED
2 teaspoons EACH OF CHOPPED PARSLEY, CHIVES
AND TARRAGON
2 tablespoons OLIVE OIL
SALT AND PEPPER
4 x 4- to 5-ounce SALMON FILLETS

Sauce
2 teaspoons CORNSTARCH
1 cup LIGHT FISH OR VEGETABLE STOCK
grated zest of 1/2 LEMON
2 tablespoons LEMON JUICE
3 tablespoons LIGHT CREAM
1 EGG YOLK
1/2 teaspoon SUGAR
1 tablespoon CHOPPED MIXED HERBS
1 tablespoon BUTTER, CUBED
1 sprig PARSLEY, TO GARNISH

Preheat the oven to 350°F. In a blender or food processor, reduce the brioche slice to crumbs. Mix with the shallot, the herbs and olive oil. Season. Place the fillets, skin sides down, on a baking tray and press the crumbs onto the tops. Set aside.

To make the sauce, mix the cornstarch with 2 tablespoons of the stock and set aside. Heat the remaining stock in a pan with the lemon zest and juice. When nearly boiling add another 2 tablespoons of the hot stock to the cornstarch. Stir, then pour the mixture into the pan. Bring to a boil, stirring constantly. Let it bubble and thicken, then lower the heat.

Bake the salmon for 6-8 minutes or until a skewer can easily be pushed through the center of the fillets. While it is baking, finish the sauce. Beat the cream and egg yolk together, then add to the pan of sauce and beat in. Stir in the sugar, herbs and, if needed, more lemon juice. Season to taste. Finally, beat in the butter. Garnish, and serve with the lemon sauce.   SERVES 4

TOP: *Salmon in Fruit and Nut Sauce*
BOTTOM: *Baked Salmon with a Brioche Crust*

Mixed Fish Cobbler

1 1/2-pound TAIL PIECE OF SALMON
1 ONION, CHOPPED
2 BAY LEAVES
PARSLEY SPRIGS
12 ounces COD FILLET
4 tablespoons BUTTER
1 tablespoon VEGETABLE OIL
2 STALKS CELERY, CHOPPED
2 LEEKS, CHOPPED
4 tablespoons ALL-PURPOSE FLOUR
2/3 cup HARD CIDER
2 tablespoons CHOPPED PARSLEY
SALT AND PEPPER
2/3 cup SOUR CREAM

Topping
2 cups SELF-RISING FLOUR
1 tablespoon CHOPPED PARSLEY
4 tablespoons BUTTER, CUBED
2/3 cup MILK
1 EGG
1 sprig PARSLEY, TO GARNISH

Cook the salmon tail with the onion, bay leaves and parsley sprigs, following the pâté recipe on page 22, but omitting the wine. Remove the salmon from the pan. Replace with the cod and poach it for 1-1^1/$_2$ minutes or until just tender. Cool both fish. Discard any bones and the skin from both fish and cut into chunks. Boil the remaining stock to reduce it to 2 cups. Strain and reserve.

Heat the butter and oil in a skillet and sauté the celery for 2 minutes. Add the leeks and cook until soft. Stir in the flour, then gradually stir in the stock and cider. Bring to a boil and stir until the sauce is smooth. Add the parsley and season. Remove from the heat and stir in the sour cream and then the fish. Spoon into a baking dish set aside.

Preheat the oven to 400°F. To make the topping, sift the flour into a bowl. Add parsley, salt and pepper and mix together. Rub in the butter with your fingertips until you have fine crumbs. Make a well in the center, pour in the milk and use a fork to mix together into a soft dough. Knead the dough lightly. Pat out the dough on a work surface, without stretching it, until it is 1/2 inch thick. Using a round cookie or biscuit cutter or the top of a glass, cut the dough into 1^1/$_2$-inch circles. Arrange the dough circles on top of the fish mixture. Beat the egg with a little salt and brush over the dough circles. Bake for 10 minutes, then reduce the heat to 350°F and continue baking for 15-20 minutes longer or until the tops are golden. Garnish with parsley. SERVES 6

RIGHT: Mixed Fish Cobbler

Fish Pie

2 tablespoons VEGETABLE OIL
1 bulb FENNEL, CHOPPED
6 SCALLIONS, CHOPPED
2 cups HALVED BUTTON MUSHROOMS
2 teaspoons GROUND CORIANDER
1 teaspoon GROUND CUMIN
3 tablespoons ALL-PURPOSE FLOUR
1 1/4 cups MILK
SALT AND PEPPER
1 pound SALMON FILLET, SKINNED AND CUT
INTO LARGE CUBES
5 ounces SHRIMP, DEFROSTED
12 ounces PIECRUST DOUGH
BEATEN EGG OR A LITTLE MILK, TO GLAZE

Heat the oil in a saucepan, then cook the fennel, covered, for 5 minutes. Add the scallions and mushrooms and cook for 1 minute, stirring. Stir in the spices and flour and cook for 1 minute longer. Slowly pour in the milk, stirring constantly. Bring to a boil and season to taste. Remove the pan from the heat and stir in the salmon and shrimp. Leave to cool.

Spoon the mixture into a 10-inch baking dish. Roll out the dough and use to cover the pie. Decorate with dough leaves cut from the trimmings. Refrigerate for 20-30 minutes. Meanwhile, preheat the oven to 375°F. Brush with egg or milk and bake for about 30 minutes or until golden on top. SERVES 6

Zucchini, Mushroom, and Salmon Bake

8 ounces ZUCCHINI
2 tablespoons VEGETABLE OIL
4 SALMON STEAKS
1 1/2 tablespoons SOY SAUCE
SALT AND PEPPER
1 1/2 cups HALVED BUTTON MUSHROOMS
1 tablespoon SNIPPED CHIVES

Preheat the oven to 350°F. Top and tail the zucchini, then cut them into batons of about 2 inches long.

Brush the inside of a baking dish or a casserole with a lid with the oil. Lightly brush the salmon steaks with some of the soy sauce and sprinkle them with pepper, then lay them in the dish in a single layer. Add the zucchini and mushrooms and drizzle with the remaining soy sauce and oil. Sprinkle some salt and pepper on and finally the chives. Cover the dish with its lid or with foil and bake for 25 minutes or until a knife will slide in easily next to the bones. Serve with rice.

SERVES 4

TOP: *Fish Pie*

BOTTOM: *Zucchini, Mushroom, and Salmon Bake*

Arancini

In Italy, these little rice balls were originally made to use up left-over risotto. Somebody then thought of stuffing them and they became a dish in their own right. Serve with Fresh Tomato Sauce (see page 18). The rice can be cooked a day in advance and stored, covered, in the refrigerator.

3 cups LIGHT CHICKEN OR VEGETABLE STOCK

1 tablespoon OIL

1 SMALL ONION, VERY FINELY CHOPPED

1 1/2 cups ARBORIO RICE

1 HANDFUL BASIL LEAVES, CHOPPED

2 tablespoons PINE NUTS, TOASTED

1 SUN-DRIED TOMATO, FINELY CHOPPED

1 tablespoon FRESHLY GRATED PARMESAN CHEESE

1 EGG, BEATEN

SALT AND PEPPER

3 ounces SALMON, SKINNED, BONED AND CUT INTO 18 CUBES

1 EGG, BEATEN

1 cup FRESH BREAD CRUMBS

EXTRA VEGETABLE OIL FOR DEEP-FRYING

Heat the stock in a pan and simmer gently. In another pan, heat the oil and cook the onion for 2 minutes, then stir in the rice. Cook, stirring, for another 2 minutes or until the rice is transparent. Stir in a ladleful of the hot stock and when it has been absorbed add another ladleful. Continue adding the stock, bit-by-bit, until the rice is tender. (Add hot water if the stock runs out.) Transfer the cooked rice to a bowl and leave to cool.

Add the chopped basil, pine nuts, sun-dried tomato, Parmesan and the egg to the rice. Mix and season well.

With wet hands, shape the mixture into 18 balls, each about the size of a golf ball. Make a hole in the side of each ball with your finger. Push a cube of salmon into the hole, then close it up.

Dip each ball into the beaten egg, then roll in the bread crumbs and, if time, refrigerate for at least 30 minutes before frying. Deep-fry over a medium heat for 7-8 minutes to ensure that the salmon is cooked. Drain well on paper towels. Serve immediately with a bowl of Fresh Tomato Sauce. SERVES 6

RIGHT: Arancini

Salmon and Tarragon en Papillote

4 *tablespoons* UNSALTED BUTTER

4 *tablespoons* OLIVE OIL

1 *pound* SALMON FILLET, SKINNED AND CUT
INTO STRIPS

1 *tablespoon* CHOPPED TARRAGON
SALT AND PEPPER

Preheat the oven to 375°F. Heat the butter and half the oil together. Sprinkle the salmon strips with the tarragon and season. Pour on the butter and oil and mix together.

Brush the four 12-inch squares of wax paper or parchment paper with the remaining oil, then place one-quarter of the mixture in the center of each. Seal them by lifting and folding together opposite sides, then folding and tucking the ends underneath.

Place the packages on a baking sheet and bake them for 8-10 minutes or until a skewer can easily be pushed through the fillets; you want to serve the fillets still enclosed in their wrappings, so test one fillet – if it is cooked through the others will be as well.   SERVES 4

Salmon and Vegetable Packages

8 *ounces* SALAD POTATOES, SLICED
SALT AND PEPPER

2 TOMATOES, PEELED, SEEDED AND
ROUGHLY CHOPPED

1 SMALL BUNCH CHIVES

5 *tablespoons* OLIVE OIL

4 SALMON STEAKS

Preheat the oven to 375°F. Boil the potatoes in a pan of salted water until just tender. Drain and rinse under cold water. Transfer to a bowl and stir in the tomatoes, chives, and 3 tablespoons of the oil. Season to taste.

Brush four 12-inch squares of wax paper or parchment paper with the remaining oil. Spoon one-quarter of the potato mixture onto each and place a salmon steak on top. Wrap, following the directions above. Bake for 15 minutes or until a knife will slide easily next to the bones. To serve, unwrap and put on individual plates.

SERVES 4

TOP: *Salmon and Tarragon en Papillote*
BOTTOM: *Salmon and Vegetable Packages*

Suppers and Snacks

For informal suppers, salmon can be cooked with rice, in kedgeree or risotto,
or served with spaghetti or in lasagne. For a light snack, strips of the fish can be mixed
with a batter and fried to make beignets, or added to eggs for a frittata.

Kedgeree

1 ¼ cups BASMATI OR OTHER LONG-GRAIN RICE

6 tablespoons BUTTER

1 tablespoon VEGETABLE OIL

1 ONION, HALVED AND THINLY SLICED

8 ounces SALMON, POACHED, BONED, SKINNED AND
FLAKED INTO LARGE PIECES

3 HARD-BOILED EGGS, CHOPPED

3 tablespoons DOUBLE CREAM

2 tablespoons CHOPPED PARSLEY

SALT AND PEPPER

Cook the rice following the directions on the package. Drain well and keep warm.

Meanwhile, make the sauce. Melt 2 tablespoons of the butter with the oil. Fry the onion until soft. Add the hot rice, the remaining butter, and all the other ingredients. Season. Cook very gently, stirring constantly, try not to break up the salmon flakes or the eggs, until the kedgeree is hot. SERVES 4

Artichoke and Mushroom Risotto

6-7 cups LIGHT CHICKEN OR VEGETABLE STOCK

1 tablespoon OLIVE OIL

6 tablespoons BUTTER

1 ONION, CHOPPED

1 ½ cups SLICED CHESTNUT MUSHROOMS

1 ½ cups ARBORIO RICE

1 X 14-ounce CAN ARTICHOKE HEARTS, DRAINED
AND HALVED

10 ounces SALMON, CUT INTO STRIPS

SALT AND PEPPER

Bring the stock to a boil and keep simmering. Heat the oil in a heavy-bottomed saucepan. Add half the butter and fry the onion until soft. Add the mushrooms to the onions and cook, stirring, for 3-4 minutes or until soft. Stir in the rice and cook until transparent. Gradually stir in the stock, waiting for one ladleful to be absorbed before adding the next. Stir constantly. When nearly all the stock has been added, stir in the artichoke hearts and salmon. Continue stirring gently.

When the rice is soft to the bite and the salmon cooked through, remove the pan from the heat. Stir in the remaining butter and season to taste. Cover and leave to stand for 3 minutes before serving. SERVES 4

RIGHT: Kedgeree

Salmon and Shrimp Crêpes

8 CRÊPES, PRECOOKED

2 tablespoons BUTTER

1 SHALLOT, CHOPPED

1 CLOVE GARLIC, CRUSHED

1/4 cup ALL-PURPOSE FLOUR

1 1/4 cups MILK

SALT AND PEPPER

8 ounces SALMON, POACHED, SKINNED, BONED
AND FLAKED

4 ounces SHELLED SMALL SHRIMP OR POPCORN
SHRIMP, DEFROSTED IF FROZEN

1 tablespoon SNIPPED CHIVES

Preheat the oven to 350°F. Interleave the crêpes with sheets of parchment or wax paper. Wrap them with foil to make one or two packages and warm them through in the oven for 10-15 minutes.

Meanwhile, melt the butter. Add the shallot and garlic and cook gently until soft. Sprinkle in the flour, stir it in and cook for a few minutes, stirring, then gradually stir in the milk. Season to taste. Bring the sauce to a boil and cook, stirring frequently, for 5 minutes. Remove from the heat and stir in the salmon and shrimp.

Remove the crêpes from the oven. Lay them flat and divide the fish mixture between them, then roll them up. Sprinkle with chives and serve immediately. SERVES 4

Spicy Fish Cakes

1 tablespoon VEGETABLE OIL

1 SMALL ONION, CHOPPED

1 teaspoon CURRY PASTE

1 1/2 cups COOKED MASHED POTATOES

12 ounces SALMON, POACHED, SKINNED, BONED
AND FLAKED

3 tablespoons CHOPPED CILANTRO

SALT AND PEPPER

2 tablespoons ALL-PURPOSE FLOUR

1 EGG, LIGHTLY BEATEN

1 1/2 cups FRESH BREAD CRUMBS

EXTRA VEGETABLE OIL FOR FRYING

Heat the oil and gently cook the onion until soft. Stir in the curry paste and cook for 1-2 minutes. Add the potatoes and stir until they are warmed through. Remove from the heat and mix in the salmon and cilantro, then season to taste. Turn the mixture onto a piece of oiled foil and refrigerate for at least 2 hours.

To cook the fish cakes, use wet hands to shape the mixture into 6-8 cakes. Dip the cakes into the flour, then the egg, then cover each with the bread crumbs. Heat the extra oil in a large skillet and fry, turning once, for 6-8 minutes or until they are golden brown. If neccessary, cook the fish cakes in batches and keep warm until the remainder are done. SERVES 4

TOP: Salmon and Shrimp Crêpes

BOTTOM: Spicy Fish Cakes

Salmon Spaghetti with a Crunchy Topping

12 ounces SPAGHETTI
7 tablespoons OLIVE OIL
1 SMALL ONION, FINELY CHOPPED
2 CLOVES GARLIC, CRUSHED
SALT AND PEPPER
8 ounces SALMON FILLET, SKINNED AND CUT INTO SMALL CUBES
2 tablespoons CHOPPED FRESH PARSLEY
1 tablespoon BUTTER
1 cup FRESH BREAD CRUMBS

Cook the spaghetti following the directions on the package.

Meanwhile, make the sauce; 2 skillets are required. In the first pan, heat half the oil and gently fry the onion and garlic. When the onion starts to soften, add the salmon and parsley. Season and fry, stirring, for 2-3 minutes longer, or until the salmon is cooked through.

At the same time heat the rest of the oil and the butter in a small skillet. Fry the bread crumbs until they are crisp and golden. Season well and drain on paper towels.

Drain the spaghetti. Transfer to a warm serving dish and immediately pour the salmon and garlic sauce over. Toss to mix, then sprinkle the bread crumbs over the top. SERVES 4

Pasta Bake

2 tablespoons BUTTER PLUS EXTRA FOR GREASING
1 tablespoon ALL-PURPOSE FLOUR
2/3 cup MILK
3 ounces DOLCELATTE CHEESE, CUT INTO SMALL CUBES
3 SUN-DRIED TOMATOES, FINELY CHOPPED
6 ounces SALMON FILLET, SKINNED AND CUT INTO SMALL CUBES
3 ounces TAGLIATELLE
SALT AND PEPPER
3 EGGS, SEPARATED
pinch CAYENNE PEPPER

Grease a $5^1/2$-cup soufflé dish. Preheat the oven to 375°F.

Melt the butter, stir in the flour and gradually add the milk. Bring to a boil, stirring constantly until the sauce is smooth. Transfer to a bowl. Stir in the cheese, sun-dried tomatoes and salmon.

Break the pasta into roughly 2-inch pieces. Cook in a large pan of salted water for about two-thirds of the time given on the packages. Drain and add to the bowl. Mix well and leave for 5 minutes to cool slightly.

Beat the egg yolks together. Add to the bowl and mix together. Season with salt and pepper and cayenne. Beat the egg whites until stiff. Fold into the mixture, then spoon it into the prepared soufflé dish. Bake for 30-35 minutes. Serve immediately. SERVES 4

TOP: *Salmon Spaghetti with a Crunchy Topping*
BOTTOM: *Pasta Bake*

Coconut Curry

Look for creamed coconut at Asian grocery stores. It is a solid mixture that comes in block form to be diluted with water. If unavailable, substitute 1¹/₄ cups coconut milk that has been strained.

8 ounces	CELLOPHANE (RICE) NOODLES
4 ounces	CREAMED COCONUT
1 tablespoon	VEGETABLE OIL
4	SCALLIONS, SLICED
2	CLOVES GARLIC, THINLY SLICED
3/4-inch piece	FRESH GINGER ROOT, PEELED AND THINLY SLICED
1 teaspoon	CURRY PASTE
small bunch	CILANTRO CHOPPED
2 teaspoons	LEMON JUICE
	SALT AND PEPEPR
4	SALMON STEAKS

Prepare the noodles following the directions on the package. They will probably only need to soak for a few minutes in very hot water.

Roughly chop the creamed coconut. Put into a bowl and pour in 1¹/₄ cups boiling water. Stir until the coconut has dissolved.

Heat the oil in a wok. Add the scallions, garlic, and ginger and stir-fry until soft. Stir in the curry paste and cook gently for 1-2 minutes. Add the coconut, cilantro, and lemon juice. Season to taste. Cook, stirring constantly, to nearly boiling point. Add the salmon steaks and cook gently for 4-5 minutes. Turn them and cook for a further 4-5 minutes or until a knife slides easily next to the bone. Serve immediately on a bed of noodles.

SERVES 4

Salmon and Snow-Pea Stir-Fry

8 ounces	SNOW-PEAS, TOPPED AND TAILED
8 ounces	BABY CORN EARS, HALVED
	SALT AND PEPPER
2 tablespoons	VEGETABLE OIL
1	ONION, ROUGHLY CHOPPED
2	CLOVES GARLIC, CHOPPED
12 ounces	SALMON FILLET, SKINNED, BONED AND CUT INTO THIN STRIPS
2-3 tablespoons	SOY SAUCE
juice of 1	LEMON

Blanch the snow-peas and baby corn in a pan of boiling salted water for 1¹/₂ minutes. Drain. Immediately run the vegetables under cold water.

Heat the oil in a wok and stir-fry the onion and garlic for 1 minute. Add the blanched vegetables and continue stir-frying for 45 seconds. Add the salmon, soy sauce, and lemon juice. Season and stir-fry for 2-2¹/₂ minutes longer or until the salmon is just cooked and a skewer can easily be pushed through the pieces. Serve immediately with rice or noodles.

SERVES 4

RIGHT: Salmon and Snow-Pea Stir-Fry

Onion and Salmon Frittata

3 tablespoons OLIVE OIL

1 large SPANISH ONION, COARSELY CHOPPED

4 EGGS

large pinch DRIED OREGANO

SALT AND PEPPER

4 ounces SALMON, POACHED, SKINNED, BONED
AND FLAKED

1 tablespoon BUTTER

In a nonstick skillet, heat 2 tablespoons of the oil and gently fry the onion, stirring frequently, for about 20 minutes or until golden. Beat the eggs and oregano together. Season. Stir in the salmon and cooked onion.

Melt the remaining oil with the butter in the skillet and when sizzling pour in the egg mixture. Cook until the bottom has set, then either turn it over or put it under the broiler to cook the other side.   SERVES 4

Beignets

4 tablespoons BUTTER

SALT AND PEPPER

1/2 cup plus 1 tablespoon ALL-PURPOSE FLOUR

2 EGGS

10 ounces SALMON FILLET, SKINNED AND CUT
INTO SMALL STRIPS

VEGETABLE OIL FOR DEEP FRYING

Put the butter in a pan with 2/3 cup water. Season. When the butter has melted, bring to a boil. Remove from the heat and immediately add the flour. Beat together, then return the pan to low heat and continue beating until the dough comes away from the sides of the pan. Cool. Beat the eggs, then gradually beat them in. Stir in the strips of salmon.

Heat the oil until a little of the pastry dropped into it sizzles immediately. Then drop in tablespoonfuls of the beignets. Fry a few at a time, turning frequently, for about 10 minutes or until they are golden. Drain on paper towels. Serve immediately.   MAKES ABOUT 20

TOP: Onion and Salmon Frittata

BOTTOM: Beignets

Fisherman's Pie

1 ¹/₂ *pounds* POTATOES, PEELED AND DICED

2 *tablespoons* BUTTER

2-3 *tablespoons* MILK

SALT AND PEPPER

2 *tablespoons* VEGETABLE OIL

1 LARGE ONION, CHOPPED

2 ¹/₂ *cups* THICKLY SLICED MUSHROOMS

1 X 10-*ounce* CAN CONDENSED CELERY SOUP

2 x 6 ¹/₈-*ounce* CANS SALMON, DRAINED, BONED AND FLAKED

Preheat the oven to 375°F. Cook the potatoes, then mash them with the butter and milk and season well.

Heat the oil and cook the onion and mushrooms until just soft. Stir in the soup, salmon, ¹/₄ cup water and season to taste. Spoon into a baking dish and cover with the mashed potatoes. Bake for 35 minutes.   SERVES 4

Lasagne

6 SHEETS READY-TO-USE LASAGNE

2 *tablespoons* PARMESAN CHEESE

Tomato Sauce

1 *tablespoon* VEGETABLE OIL

1 ONION, FINELY CHOPPED

2 CLOVES GARLIC, CRUSHED

1 X 14-*ounce* CAN CRUSHED TOMATOES

1 TEASPOON DRIED HERBES DE PROVENCE

²/₃ *cup* SOUR CREAM

8 *ounces* SALMON, POACHED, BONED, SKINNED AND FLAKED

Cheese Sauce

3 *tablespoons* BUTTER

¹/₄ *cup* ALL-PURPOSE FLOUR

2 ¹/₂ *cups* MILK

1 ¹/₂ *cups* GRATED SHARP CHEDDAR CHEESE

Preheat the oven to 350°F. To make the tomato sauce, heat the oil and sauté the onion and garlic until soft. Stir in the tomatoes and herbs. Season to taste. Bring to a boil, then simmer gently for 10-15 minutes or until the sauce has thickened. Cool. Stir in the sour cream and salmon.

To make the cheese sauce, melt the butter. Stir in the flour and cook for 1 minute. While gradually stirring, pour in the milk. Bring to a boil. Remove from the heat, cool slightly, then stir in three-quarters of the cheese. Season. Spoon half the tomato sauce into a buttered oblong baking dish and place 3 sheets of lasagne over it. Spoon half the cheese sauce over and repeat the layers. Sprinkle the remaining cheese over the top, then dredge with the Parmesan. Cover with greased foil and bake for 30 minutes. Remove the foil and bake for 20 minutes longer to brown the top.   SERVES 4

RIGHT: Lasagne

Entertaining

A whole, decorated salmon is an eye-catching centerpiece for any special occasion or party. Plain or flavored, homemade mayonnaise is the perfect accompaniment. Salmon adds an air of sophistication to entertaining any number of guests.

Whole Salmon Baked with Wine and Herbs

1 x 4- to 5-pound SALMON, DRAWN, SCALED AND RINSED
SALT AND PEPPER
several sprigs PARSLEY, TARRAGON AND CHERVIL
1 LEMON, THINLY SLICED
6 tablespoons BUTTER, MELTED
1 1/4 cups WHITE WINE

Sauce
1 1/4 cups LIGHT CREAM
2 tablespoons BUTTER

Preheat the oven to 325°F. Sprinkle the salmon with salt and pepper, both inside and out. Put one or two sprigs of each herb and the lemon slices inside the fish.

Brush one side of a very large sheet of foil with melted butter. Put some herb sprigs and lemon slices down the center and place the salmon on top. Draw up the sides of foil. Drizzle the remaining butter over the fish. Place a few more sprigs of herbs and the remaining lemon slices on top. Pour the wine over. Make a loose package by bringing up the sides and folding them together. Repeat with the ends. Ensure the package is well sealed. Carefully transfer to a baking sheet and bake for 1 hour.

Remove from the oven, snip off a corner of foil and tip the baking sheet to drain the juices into a saucepan. Bring to a boil and boil until reduced by half. Stir in the cream. When it bubbles, simmer until the sauce thickens. While the sauce is simmering, undo the top of the package. Use a blunt-ended knife to remove the skin and fins. Use the foil to turn the salmon onto a serving platter. Remove the remaining skin and fins. Carefully scrape away any dark pieces of flesh, if you wish.

To finish the sauce, stir in the butter and season. Serve immediately, accompanied by the sauce, or keep warm by covering loosely with the foil.   SERVES 6-8

RIGHT: Whole Salmon Baked with Wine and Herbs

Mayonnaise

It is not difficult to make mayonnaise, and when it is freshly made it is particularly delicious with chilled salmon. For a party, serve three bowls of mayonnaise with different flavors and colors.

2 EGG YOLKS
1 tablespoon LEMON JUICE
1 1/4 cups OLIVE OIL
SALT AND PEPPER

Beat the egg yolks and lemon juice together. Beat constantly, adding the oil drop-by-drop. Ensure the oil has been incorporated in the egg yolk before adding the next drop. When the mayonnaise starts to thicken and about half the oil has been used, start adding the oil more quickly, teaspoon-by-teaspoon. Season. Dilute, if necessary, with a few more drops of lemon juice.

For Herb Mayonnaise, stir in 3 tablespoons of chopped fresh herbs (parsley, tarragon, chervil, chives). For Mango and Cilantro Mayonnaise, substitute half the olive oil with sunflower oil. Add the mashed flesh of half a mango and 1 tablespoon of chopped fresh cilantro.

Chilled Decorated Salmon

Follow the recipe for the whole baked salmon on page 64, but use oil instead of butter and omit the wine – the salmon will cook in its own juices. Any remaining aspic can be chopped, then spooned around the chilled fish.

1 x 4- to 5-pound SALMON, DRAWN, SCALED AND RINSED
3 tablespoons VEGETABLE OIL
several sprigs PARSLEY, TARRAGON AND CHERVIL
1 LEMON, THINLY SLICED

1 LARGE OR 2 SMALL CUCUMBERS
1 ENVELOPE ASPIC POWDER (SEE PAGE 24)

Leave the salmon to cool in the foil. Skin and wrap loosely in a clean piece of foil. Refrigerate for 2 hours or leave in a cold place for 3 hours, or chill in the freezer for 30 minutes. Retain the foil.

Peel the cucumbers, leaving a few narrow stripes of skin. Slice very thinly. Place in a colander, sprinkle with salt and leave for 30 minutes. Rinse with cold water, then turn onto a dish towel. Pat dry and chill for 30 minutes.

Make the aspic following the directions on the package. Leave until syrupy. Use the foil to roll the salmon onto a serving dish. Starting at the tail end, arrange the cucumber slices to resemble scales. Brush a layer of almost-set aspic over the cucumber slices. Leave to set. Brush on another layer and, if necessary, a third. Leave in a cold place to set.   SERVES 6-8

TOP: Herb Mayonnaise, Mayonnaise, Mango Mayonnaise
BOTTOM: Chilled Decorated Salmon

Spinach and Salmon in Pastry

Sauce Mousseline is a light version of Hollandaise Sauce.

1 ³/₄ pounds FROZEN SPINACH
6 tablespoons HEAVY CREAM
1 EGG YOLK
4 tablespoons FRESH BREAD CRUMBS
pinch GRATED NUTMEG
SALT AND PEPPER
1 pound STORE-BOUGHT PUFF PASTRY, DEFROSTED IF NECESSARY
4-5 tablespoons SEMOLINA
1 x 4- to 5-pound SALMON, FILLETED AND SKINNED
1 EGG, BEATEN

Sauce
1 quantity HOLLANDAISE SAUCE, PAGE 36
²/₃ cup HEAVY CREAM, WHIPPED

Preheat the oven to 425°F. Cook the spinach following the directions on the package. Drain well, squeezing out as much water as possible. Purée in a blender or food processor, then place in a bowl and stir in the cream, egg yolk and bread crumbs. Season with nutmeg and salt and pepper.

Divide the pastry dough in half and roll out one half very thinly into a large rectangle. Trim, so that the pastry measures 1¹/2 inches larger all around than a fillet. Place the pastry on a baking sheet and prick all over with a fork. Bake for 20 minutes, turning it over half way through. Keep the oven on.

Remove the pastry from the oven and turn it over again. Cool slightly. Dredge with the semolina. Lay one salmon fillet on top, spread with the spinach and lay the other fillet on top, turned head to tail.

Roll out the remaining pastry into a large rectangle measuring 1¹/2 inches larger than the base all around. Brush the edges with beaten egg and cover the salmon, tucking in the edges underneath. Use a teaspoon to make scales and use the pastry trimmings to make leaves. Make 4 small slits in the top and brush all over with egg. Bake for 25 minutes, then reduce the temperature to 350°F for a further 25 minutes longer.

Meanwhile, make the sauce. Stir the cream into the Hollandaise. Adjust the seasoning and dilute if necessary, with a little more lemon juice. Serve the salmon very hot with the sauce. SERVES 8-10

RIGHT: Spinach and Salmon in Pastry

Ginger and Raisin Filo Pastry Packages

1/2 cup RAISINS

1 1/2 tablespoons BRANDY

3 PIECES OF STEM GINGER FROM A JAR OF GINGER IN SYRUP, DRAINED

grated zest and juice of 1 LEMON

SALT AND PEPPER

3/4 cup BUTTER

6 x 4- to 5-ounce SALMON FILLETS, SKINNED

9 ounces STORE-BOUGHT FILO PASTRY: TWELVE 10 1/2- X 9 1/2- INCH SHEETS

Sauce

2 SHALLOTS, VERY FINELY CHOPPED

6 tablespoons WHITE WINE

6 tablespoons WHITE-WINE VINEGAR

1 1/2 cups VERY COLD UNSALTED BUTTER

1 tablespoon HEAVY CREAM

1 1/2 tablespoons SYRUP FROM THE GINGER JAR

Soak the raisins in the brandy and lemon juice for several hours or overnight.

Finely chop the ginger. Mash with the lemon zest and salt and pepper into half the butter. Stir in the brandy and raisins. Divide the mixture between the salmon fillets and spread over the tops.

Preheat the oven to 400°F. Melt the remaining butter. Lightly brush a sheet of pastry dough with butter. Top with another one and brush with butter. Place a salmon fillet in the center. Fold 4 small triangles in at each corner, then bring the longer sides up and over the fish. Fold up the ends to make a neat package. Seal the edges with a little more butter and place the package, seam side down, on a lightly greased baking sheet. Make 5 more packages in the same way. Brush the tops with butter and bake for 20-25 minutes or until the pastry is golden and crisp.

For the sauce, put the shallots, wine and vinegar into a heavy-bottomed pan. Bring to a boil. Simmer until the liquid is reduced to about 1 tablespoon. Reduce the heat to very low. Cut the butter into cubes. Beat in the cream and, one-by-one, the cubes of butter. If the sauce shows any sign of separating remove the pan from the heat and, if necessary, beat in an ice cube. When all the butter has been added, turn up the heat. Bring to a boil. Strain out the shallot, then stir in the ginger syrup and season.

The sauce can be kept warm for up to 30 minutes by putting it in a bowl over a pan of just-simmering water.

SERVES 6

RIGHT: Ginger and Raisin Filo Pastry Package

Chaudfroid of Salmon

4 x 4- to 5-ounce PIECES SALMON FILLET, POACHED

1 large pinch SAFFRON

1 1/4 cups MAYONNAISE, PREFERABLY HOMEMADE

1 1/2 teaspoons UNFLAVORED GELATIN

4 sprigs TARRAGON

LETTUCE LEAVES, TO SERVE

Chill the cooked salmon for at least 1 hour. Meanwhile, put the saffron into 2 teaspoons of very hot water and leave to soak for 10 minutes. Stir into the mayonnaise. Leave to cool.

Skin the salmon and place the fillets on a wire rack. Dissolve the gelatin following the directions on the package in 1 tablespoon of water. Stir into the mayonnaise.

Spoon the setting mayonnaise over the salmon. Place a tarragon sprig on each fillet. Leave until set. Serve on a bed of lettuce.   SERVES 4

RIGHT: Chaudfroid of Salmon

Outdoor Eating

When the weather is warm, informal meals are enjoyable out of doors. Salmon steaks can be cooked on the barbecue and eaten with salsa. A salmon tart or club sandwiches can be packed up and taken on picnics.

Avocado and Tomato Salsa

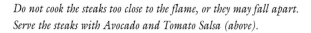

grated zest and juice of 2 LIMES
SALT AND PEPPER
1/2 RED ONION, FINELY CHOPPED
4 TOMATOES, PEELED AND SEEDED
1 AVOCADO

Mix the lime zest and juice together and season. Add the onion. Dice the tomatoes and add to the bowl. Quarter the avocado. Remove the stone and skin, then dice the flesh. Add to the bowl and toss carefully. Cover and chill until ready to serve.   SERVES 4

Barbecued Salmon Steaks

Do not cook the steaks too close to the flame, or they may fall apart.
Serve the steaks with Avocado and Tomato Salsa (above).

4 x 6- to 7-ounce SALMON STEAKS
OLIVE OIL
CHOPPED FRESH CILANTRO

When the coals are glowing, brush the steaks with oil and put them into a fish rack or holder. The cooking time depends on the heat of the coals and the thickness of the salmon, but turn them after 3 minutes and check after another 3 minutes. Sprinkle with cilantro.

Club Sandwich

7 tablespoons MAYONNAISE
2 teaspoons MANGO CHUTNEY
6 SLICES BREAD, TOASTED
4-6 SMALL LETTUCE LEAVES
1 TOMATO, PEELED AND SLICED
2 SLICES CRISP BACON, CRUMBLED
4 ounces SALMON, POACHED, SKINNED, BONED
AND FLAKED
1/2 AVOCADO, SLICED

Mix 2 tablespoons of the mayonnaise with the chutney and spread on 2 pieces of toast. Add a few lettuce leaves, cover with the tomato slices and sprinkle with bacon. Spread 2 more pieces of toast with mayonnaise, cover with salmon and then avocado. Place, salmon side up, on the prepared pieces. Spread the final pieces of toast with mayonnaise and put them on top. Secure with toothpicks. Cut into triangles.   MAKES 2

TOP: Avocado and Tomato Salsa
BOTTOM: Barbecued Salmon Steaks

Salmon Fillets with Fruity Barbecue Sauce

Any remaining barbecue sauce can be served on the side.

1/2-inch PIECE FRESH GINGER ROOT, PEELED AND
ROUGHLY CHOPPED
1 CLOVE GARLIC, ROUGHLY CHOPPED
2/3 cup TOMATO CATSUP
1 tablespoon VEGETABLE OIL
grated zest and juice of 1 ORANGE
1 tablespoon LIGHT BROWN SUGAR
4- to 5-ounce PIECES SALMON FILLET WITH THE SKIN ON
PER PERSON

To make the sauce, put all the other ingredients except the salmon in a blender or food processor and process until well blended. Transfer to a bowl and set aside for at least 2 hours.

An hour before cooking, generously brush the flesh side of the fish with the sauce; set aside.

Put the pieces of fillet into a wire fish rack. Cook the fish, flesh side down, over glowing coals. After about 3 minutes turn it over, brush the top with a little more sauce and grill for 3-4 minutes longer or until a skewer can easily be pushed through the center of the fillets.

SERVES 2-4

Barbecued Salmon with Citrus

A middle cut of salmon cooks evenly on the barbecue if wrapped in foil. Slash the sides so the smoke flavors the fish.

8-10 KUMQUATS OR
1-2 ORANGES
4 tablespoons BUTTER, PREFERABLY UNSALTED
2 tablespoons CHOPPED DILL
2 CLOVES GARLIC, CRUSHED
SALT AND PEPPER
2- to 3-pound PIECE OF MIDDLE-CUT SALMON

Slice the kumquats or, if using oranges, cut off the tops and bottoms and then cut in half from top to bottom and slice. Mix the butter, dill and garlic together and season. Layer 2 large sheets of foil together

Stuff the salmon with half the butter mixture and half the kumquat or orange slices. Spread half the remaining butter over one-half of the foil and arrange half the remaining kumquat or orange slices on it. Place the salmon on top of the butter and fruit slices. Spread the remaining butter over the top of the fish and place the remaining kumquat or orange slices on it.

Bring the unbuttered side of the foil up over the fish and make a loose package, tightly sealed on one side. Make three 2-to 3-inch angled slashes in the foil on both sides. Place on a rack over a good quantity of glowing coals. Keep the coals very hot and cook for 15-20 minutes a side. To test if cooked, partly open the package. Use a fork to check that the salmon flesh easily comes away from the bone.

SERVES 4-6

TOP: Salmon Fillets with Fruity Barbecue Sauce

BOTTOM: Barbecued Salmon with Citrus

Asparagus and Salmon Tart

4 *ounces* ASPARAGUS TIPS

SALT AND PEPPER

PREPARED PIECRUST DOUGH FOR
AN 8-INCH TART

8 *ounces* SALMON, POACHED, SKINNED, BONED
AND FLAKED

3 EGGS

2/3 cup LIGHT CREAM

2 SCALLIONS, CHOPPED

Trim the asparagus. Cook in boiling salted water for 3 minutes, or until tender. Drain and immediately run under cold water. Cut the stalks diagonally in half.

Preheat the oven to 400°F. Roll out the dough and use to line an 8-inch loose-bottomed tart pan. Prick the bottom with a fork and fill with a large piece of crumpled foil. Put on a baking sheet and bake for 15 minutes. Remove from the oven. Turn the temperature down to 350°F.

Remove and discard the foil. Lay the pieces of asparagus and the salmon in the tart shell. Mix the eggs and cream together, then stir in the onions and season. Pour over the salmon and asparagus and return the tart to the oven to bake for 35-40 minutes longer or until the top is golden and the filling is set. Serve warm or cool.

SERVES 4-6

Barbecued Stuffed Potatoes

2 *tablespoons* BUTTER

6 POTATOES

1 x 6 1/8-ounce CAN RED SALMON, BONED AND FLAKED

3 *tablespoons* HEAVY CREAM

2 *tablespoons* SNIPPED CHIVES

Melt the butter, then brush it over each potato and sprinkle them with salt. Wrap each potato in a generous square of foil. Put in the middle of hot barbecue coals and leave to cook for 50 minutes. Remove, using a long pair of tongs. Leave to cool slightly.

Partially unwrap the potatoes and, wearing a pair of oven mitts, cut off the top and scoop out most of the potato. Mash about two-thirds of the cooked potato until smooth. Stir in all the other ingredients and spoon the mixture back into the potatoes. Wrap them up again; a new layer of foil may be needed. Return to the coals for another 10 minutes.

SERVES 6

TOP: *Asparagus and Salmon Tart*
BOTTOM: *Barbecued Stuffed Potatoes*

Microwave Dishes

The microwave poaches salmon steaks or pieces of fillet perfectly. They can be eaten hot with a sauce or butter, or cold with mayonnaise. Additional tips for cooking salmon in a microwave begin on page 11 of the Introduction.

How to Microwave Salmon Steaks, Fillets or a Tail Piece

2 x 6- to 7-ounce SALMON STEAKS
2 x 5- to 6-ounce SALMON FILLETS
1 x 1-pound SALMON TAIL PIECE

For best results, arrange the fish so the thickest part is to the outside in a shallow microwave-safe dish. In a 650 watt microwave, the steaks will take 4^1/2 minutes on High (100%); the fillets will take 3^1/2 minutes on High; the tail piece will take 5 minutes on High.

Flavored Butters

These tasty butters chill quickly and release their flavors when they melt over hot salmon. Serve in pats on freshly-cooked steaks or fillets.

Parsley Butter
4 tablespoons BUTTER, SOFTENED
2 tablespoons CHOPPED FRESH PARSLEY
1 teaspoon LEMON JUICE
SALT AND PEPPER

Mash all the ingredients together. Season to taste. Shape into a 1-inch thick roll, then wrap in foil and chill. Cut the cold butter into 4 pats and serve on top of hot salmon.

Tarragon and Garlic Butter
4 tablespoons BUTTER, SOFTENED
1 tablespoon CHOPPED TARRAGON
1 clove GARLIC, CRUSHED

Mash all the ingredients together. Shape, chill and serve as above.

Orange and Mustard Butter
2 teaspoons DIJON MUSTARD
1 teaspoon ORANGE JUICE
4 tablespoons BUTTER, SOFTENED
grated zest of ^{1}/2 ORANGE

Mix the mustard and orange juice together. Mash in the butter, zest and season to taste. Shape, chill and serve as above.

RIGHT: Salmon Fillets with Flavored Butters

Salmon Steaks with Hazelnut Sauce

2 x 6- to 7-ounce SALMON STEAKS
1 tablespoon STOCK OR WINE
2 tablespoons TOASTED HAZELNUTS AND VERY FINELY CHOPPED HAZELNUTS
4 tablespoons CRÈME FRAÎCHE OR SOUR CREAM
1 tablespoon MANGO CHUTNEY

Put the steaks into a microwave-safe dish, sprinkle in the stock or wine and cook for $4^1/2$ minutes on High (100%) or until a knife will slide in easily next to the bone. Remove and keep warm. Stir all the other ingredients together in the bowl, then partially cover and microwave on High for 2 minutes. Serve the steaks on hot plates with the sauce poured over them. SERVES 2

Rolled Sole and Salmon with Parsley Sauce

2 tablespoons BUTTER
2 FILLETS LEMON SOLE, SKINNED
SALT AND PEPPER
2 x 2-ounce pieces SALMON FILLET, SKINNED
2 tablespoons WHITE WINE

Parsley Sauce
2/3 cup MILK
1 teaspoon CORNSTARCH
2 tablespoons CHOPPED PARSLEY
SALT AND PEPPER
2 tablespoons HEAVY CREAM

Put the butter in a small microwave-safe dish and melt in the microwave on Medium (50%) for 30 seconds. Brush the inside of each lemon sole fillet with melted butter, then lightly sprinkle with salt and pepper. Place a piece of salmon fillet near one end and roll up. Secure with a toothpick and brush the outsides of the rolls with the remaining butter. Put into a microwave-safe dish, sprinkle in the wine, cover and microwave on High (100%) for 3 minutes. Check that the salmon is cooked through and that a skewer can easily be pushed through the center of the fillets and, if necessary, microwave for a further 30 minutes-1 minute. Keep the fish warm.

To make the sauce, stir 2 tablespoons of the milk into the cornstarch. When smooth, gradually stir in the rest of the milk and the fish juices from the dish. Stir in the parsley and season. Return the sauce to the dish, cover and microwave on High for 4 minutes, stirring once or twice during cooking. Stir in the cream and serve with the fish rolls. SERVES 2

TOP: *Salmon Steaks with Hazelnut Sauce*
BOTTOM: *Rolled Sole and Salmon with Parsley Sauce*

Quick Pasta Sauce

A quick-and-easy sauce to pour over bowls of freshly cooked pasta.

2 teaspoons CORNSTARCH
2/3 cup MILK
1 small ONION, ROUGHLY CHOPPED
1 clove GARLIC
1 x 6 1/8-ounce CAN RED SALMON, SKIN AND BONES
DISCARDED
2/3 cup LIGHT CREAM
1 tablespoon CHOPPED DILL
SALT AND PEPPER

Mix the cornstarch to a paste with 1 tablespoon of the milk, then, stirring slowly, pour in the remaining milk.

Chop the onion and garlic in a blender or food processor. Add the salmon and purée, then slowly add the milk and cornstarch mixture through the feed tube. Transfer to a microwave-safe bowl or measuring jug, stir in the cream and dill and season. Microwave on High (100%) for about 4 minutes. Stir 2 or 3 times during cooking. To serve, pour over hot pasta. SERVES 4

Salmon and Shrimp Pâté

---

2 x 5-ounce SALMON STEAKS
1/2 cup BUTTER
1 tablespoon SHERRY
pinch GROUND MACE OR GRATED NUTMEG
SALT AND PEPPER
4 ounces SHELLED SHRIMP, DEFROSTED IF FROZEN

Cook the salmon as described on page 11. Remove the skin and any bones, then flake the flesh into a bowl. Put the butter in a small microwave-safe bowl. Partially cover and melt in the microwave on Medium (50%) for 30 seconds; set aside.

Mash the salmon, then stir in the sherry, mace and melted butter. Season. Stir until fairly smooth. Roughly chop the shrimp and add to the mixture. Spoon into a small dish, cover and chill for 2-3 hours.

To keep the pâté for 2-3 days, seal it by pouring an extra 2 tablespoons melted butter over the top.

SERVES 4

TOP: *Quick Pasta Sauce*
BOTTOM: *Salmon and Shrimp Pâté*

Smoked Salmon and Gravadlax

A luxury food for any meal, smoked salmon is also a convenience food; it comes ready to eat. It can be wrapped around various stuffings, added to mousses or tossed into plates of pasta. Gravadlax, Scandinavian in origin, can be made at home.

Smoked Salmon — How to Serve It

For a first course:
7-10 ounces SMOKED SALMON, SLICED
2 LEMONS, QUARTERED
BLACK PEPPER AND CAYENNE PEPPER
8 *slices* WHOLE-WHEAT BREAD
BUTTER, SOFTENED

Lay the salmon slices on individual plates and garnish each with 2 quarters of lemon. The diners can squeeze their own lemon juice over the fish and sprinkle it with black pepper and a little cayenne.

Serve with whole-wheat bread and butter. SERVES 4

Individual Smoked Salmon Salads

2 HARD-BOILED EGGS, CHOPPED
2 *tablespoons* MAYONNAISE
8 *ounces* SMOKED SALMON, SLICED
16 *spears* ASPARAGUS, COOKED
4 *slices* BUTTERED WHOLE-WHEAT BREAD

Mix the eggs with the mayonnaise. Season. Divide the mixture between 4 plates, spooning into mounds on one side of each plate. Divide the salmon between each plate. Arrange 4 asparagus spears beside the salmon. Add slices of bread cut into 4 triangles. Garnish with lemon wedges.

SERVES 4

Stuffed Avocados

1/2 RED BELL PEPPER, BROILED AND PEELED
1 *tablespoon* WHITE-WINE VINEGAR
3 *tablespoons* SUNFLOWER OIL
2 *tablespoons* OLIVE OIL
1/4 cup LONG-GRAIN RICE, COOKED
4 *ounces* SMOKED SALMON, CUT INTO STRIPS
2 LARGE, RIPE AVOCADOS

Cut the pepper flesh into strips. Mix the vinegar with the oils. Season well. Pour the dressing over the rice and toss well, then stir in the salmon and pepper. Halve the avocados, remove the seeds and fill the hollow with the mixture. SERVES 4

TOP: *Individual Smoked Salmon Salads*
BOTTOM: *Stuffed Avocados*

Smoked Salmon Pinwheels

These bite-sized snacks are ideal for passing around at a party.

1 tablespoon CHOPPED DILL
1 teaspoon LEMON JUICE
1 tablespoon BUTTER, SOFTENED
4-5 thin slices WHOLE-WHEAT BREAD
4 ounces SMOKED SALMON, SLICED
PEPPER

In a small bowl, mash the dill and lemon juice into the butter. Cut the crusts from the bread, then butter the slices with the flavored butter. Lay the smoked salmon on the bread, cutting off any edges and using the pieces to fill in any gaps. Leave one end of the bread uncovered. Sprinkle the pepper over. Roll up the bread, starting at the end opposite the uncovered one. Use a sharp knife to cut each into 4 or 5 pinwheels.

MAKES 20-25

Smoked Salmon Canapés

4-5 slices WHOLE-WHEAT BREAD
4 ounces SMOKED SALMON, SLICED
PARSLEY BUTTER OR
TARRAGON AND GARLIC BUTTER (SEE PAGE 80)

Place the smoked salmon on whole-wheat bread spread with a Flavored Butter (see page 80), then cut the bread into squares or rectangles. For Christmas or special occasions, use a cookie cutter to make stars, and decorate with a little chopped dill sprinkled over the points.

MAKES 20-25

Smoked Salmon Pillows

Taramasalata is a pale pink dip made from fish roe that was originally from Greece. Look for it sold in tubs at your supermarket delicatessen counter, or freshly prepared in gourmet food stores.

4 ounces TARAMASALATA
1/2 cup CREAM CHEESE
4 large thin slices SMOKED SALMON
8 CHIVES
LEMON WEDGES
8 slices PUMPERNICKEL BREAD, BUTTERED

Mix the taramasalata and cream cheese together. Divide between the smoked salmon slices, then fold over the edges and shape into round pillows. Tie 2 chives around each and serve with wedges of lemon and buttered pumpernickel.

SERVES 4

TOP: *Smoked Salmon Pinwheels, Smoked Salmon Canapés*
BOTTOM: *Smoked Salmon Pillows*

Smoked Salmon with Shrimp and Grapes

6 ounces SMOKED SALMON, SLICED

6 ounces SEEDLESS GRAPES

6 ounces SHELLED SHRIMP, DEFROSTED IF FROZEN

2 tablespoons MAYONNAISE

SALT AND PEPPER

Line 4 ramekins with the slices of smoked salmon, leaving the edges hanging over the sides. Reserve 4 small sprigs of grapes and about one-quarter of the shrimp. Pick the rest of the grapes from their stems and mix, with the remaining shrimp, into the mayonnaise. Season if necessary. Spoon the mixture into the ramekins, and fold the flaps of smoked salmon over the tops. Chill for at least 1 hour.

Run a round-bladed knife around the inside of each ramekin and carefully unmold out onto individual plates. Garnish with the reserved grapes and shrimp.

SERVES 4

Smoked Salmon with Ricotta and Herbs

6 ounces SMOKED SALMON, SLICED

1/2 small clove GARLIC

SALT AND PEPPER

1 cup RICOTTA CHEESE

4-5 tablespoons CHOPPED PARSLEY

2 tablespoons SNIPPED CHIVES

Line 4 ramekins with smoked salmon, as above. Crush the garlic with a little salt, then mix it with the ricotta and herbs. Season to taste.

Spoon the mixture into the ramekins and fold the flaps of smoked salmon over the top. Chill for at least 1 hour. Run a round-bladed knife around the inside of each ramekin and carefully unmold onto individual plates. Garnish with a few sprigs of parsley and a wedge of lemon. Serve with whole-wheat bread and butter.

SERVES 4

RIGHT: Smoked Salmon with Shrimp and Grapes

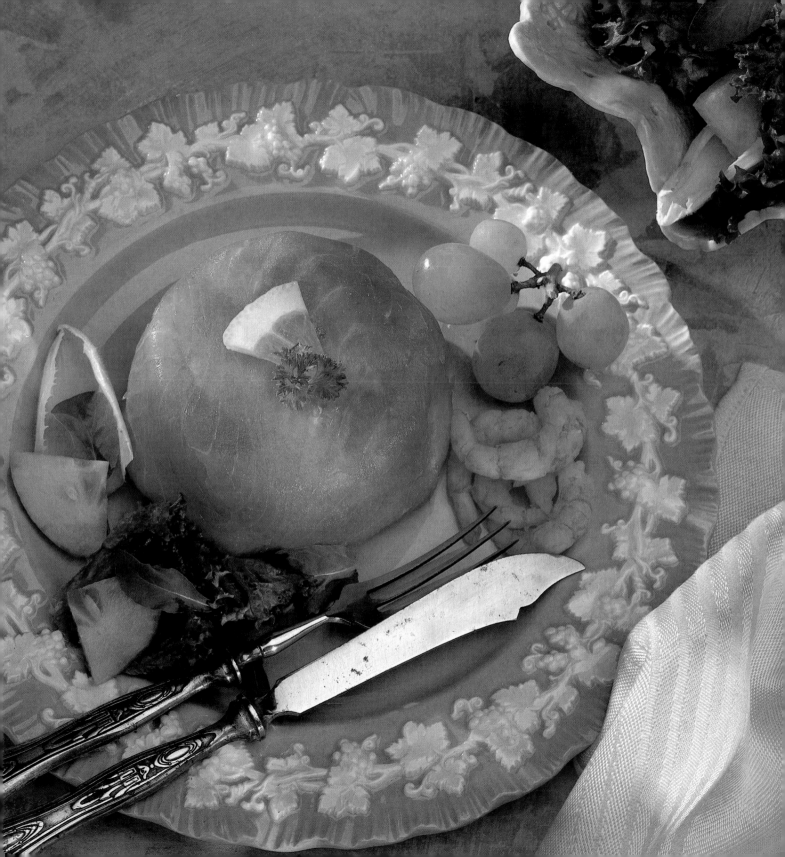

Tagliatelle with Smoked Salmon and Arugula

12 ounces TAGLIATELLE
4 tablespoons BUTTER, CUT INTO SMALL CUBES
2/3 cup HEAVY CREAM
8 ounces SMOKED SALMON, ROUGHLY CHOPPED
1 small bunch ARUGULA, CHOPPED
SALT AND PEPPER

Turn the oven onto its low setting. Cook the pasta following the directions on the package.

Meanwhile, in a bowl large enough to hold the cooked pasta, put the butter and cream; warm it in the oven.

Drain the pasta and transfer it to the warmed bowl. Add the salmon, arugula, a good grinding of pepper and toss to mix well. Add salt if necessary. SERVES 4

Sour Cream and Smoked Salmon Pizzas

2/3 cup SOUR CREAM
finely shredded zest and juice of 1 LEMON
SALT AND PEPPER
4 x 3-ounce STORE-BOUGHT PIZZA BASES, BAKED
8 ounces SMOKED SALMON, SLICED
1 tablespoon CHOPPED DILL

Mix the sour cream with 1 teaspoon lemon juice. Season to taste. Spread the pizzas with about half of the sour cream, then arrange the salmon slices on the top. Spread the rest of the sour cream over, filling in any gaps in the middle or around the edge of the salmon. Decorate with the dill and shreds of lemon zest.

SERVES 4

Smoked Salmon Pots

8 ounces SMOKED SALMON, SLICED
1 cup MARSCAPONE OR CREAM CHEESE
1 tablespoon CHOPPED DILL
SALT AND PEPPER
1 teaspoon UNFLAVORED GELATIN
4 tablespoons LEMON JUICE
4 ounces SMOKED SALMON PIECES, ROUGHLY CHOPPED
1 sprig DILL, TO GARNISH

Line 4 oiled ramekins with smoked salmon slices, leaving the edges hanging over the sides. Mash the marscapone with the dill and season. Dissolve the gelatin, following the directions on the package, in the lemon juice. Stir into the marscapone mixture. Quickly, before the gelatin sets, stir in the salmon pieces. Spoon the mixture into the ramekins, and fold the flaps of smoked salmon over the tops. Chill for at least 1 hour. Run a round-bladed knife around the inside of each ramekin and carefully unmold onto individual plates, top with a sprig of dill and serve. SERVES 4

TOP: Tagliatelle with Smoked Salmon and Arugula
BOTTOM: Sour Cream and Smoked Salmon Pizzas

Gravadlax with Dill and Mustard Sauce

1 x 4-pound WHOLE SALMON, FILLETED

3 tablespoons SALT

2 tablespoons SUGAR

2 teaspoons PEPPER

1 large bunch DILL

1 LEMON, SLICED

LETTUCE LEAVES

Dill and Mustard Sauce

2 tablespoons DIJON MUSTARD

1 tablespoon WINE VINEGAR

1 tablespoon SUGAR

6 tablespoons SUNFLOWER OIL

1 tablespoon CHOPPED DILL

SALT AND PEPPER

Choose a dish that is long enough for the salmon to lie in flat. Mix the salt, sugar and pepper together. Put 1 salmon fillet, skin side down, in the dish. Sprinkle half the salt mixture over it and cover with a thick layer of dill. Sprinkle on the remaining salt mixture, then place the other fillet on top; head to tail and skin side up. Any left-over dill can be strewn over the top. Cover with a double layer of foil. Put a board on the top and approximately 4 pounds of cans on the board. Leave in the bottom of the refrigerator for 3 days, turning the salmon and basting with the juices twice a day.

After 3 days, discard the herbs and juices and pat the fish all over with paper towels to remove any excess salt. Wrap in foil and refrigerate until ready to serve.

For the sauce, mix the mustard, vinegar and sugar together. Gradually beat in the oil. Stir in the dill and season. Lay the fish on a dish, and surround with lettuce leaves and lemon slices. SERVES 4

Citrus-Flavored Gravadlax

1 x 4-pound WHOLE SALMON, FILLETED

3 tablespoons SALT

2 tablespoons SUGAR

1 teaspoon PEPPER

grated zest of 1 large ORANGE

grated zest of 1/2 LEMON

1 small bunch THYME

Orange and Honey Sauce

1 EGG YOLK

1 teaspoon DIJON MUSTARD

2 tablespoons ORANGE JUICE

6 tablespoons SUNFLOWER OIL

grated zest of 1/2 ORANGE

1 tablespoon HONEY

Prepare the fish and marinate in exactly the same way as Gravadlax with Dill and Mustard Sauce (above), but replace the dill with the lemon zest and the thyme.

To make the orange and honey sauce, beat the egg yolk with the mustard and half the orange juice. Slowly drip in the oil, beating constantly. When the sauce has amalgamated, stir in the remaining ingredients.

Serve the salmon with whole-wheat bread and butter or boiled potatoes, accompanied by the sauce. SERVES 4

TOP: Gravadlax with Dill and Mustard Sauce; Citrus-Flavored Gravadlax

BOTTOM: Gravadlax

Index